The Iron Spirit

The Iron Spirit

GoGo Sof

Edited By: Christopher Chng

PARTRIDGE

ISBN: Hardcover   978-1-4828-6490-8
           Softcover   978-1-4828-6491-5
           eBook   978-1-4828-6492-2

Print information available on the last page.

To order additional copies of this book, contact
Toll Free 800 101 2657 (Singapore)
Toll Free 1 800 81 7340 (Malaysia)
orders.singapore@partridgepublishing.com

www.partridgepublishing.com/singapore

To my mum and dad
    Who provided me with a strong heart and healthy mind. I am your
    daughter, and will always be.

To my husband, Richard:
    Thank you for selflessly accepting me as who I am and continuously
    giving me the opportunity to inspire others.

To Christopher Chng:
    Who has spent many hours proofing and editing the book to
    make sure my story is as accurate as it should be. Thank you for
    believing in me.

Last but not least, to *all my teammates:*
    Who have walked along this journey with me, for helping me to
    achieve my goals.

Thanks to everyone for reading my story and getting to know who I
really am beyond the petite girl you see at the races.

Contents

PART 3
EMBRACING LIFE

Preface

It seems incredible that I would be penning down my personal story, sharing the life of what a petite girl like me did, and for the reasons she feels worth doing so. It always makes me smile to think of all those people who believed in me and supported me.

And in the last few years, my wonderful husband, Richard, has given his advice and support for every step I have taken in my life.

Everyday I meet people and I am thankful for the feedback, sharings, and anecdotes I receive.

It was ten years ago whilst I was running with a colleague that I saw her potential, in terms of her working spirit and her running passion. So I asked her to work towards completing a marathon, to which she said that she would do so one day. She was so inspired by how I had been literally living the sport, and suggested to me to write a blog, a book, or something. Last year, she completed her first marathon!

And few years ago, I signed up my fifty-year-old junior colleague for a vertical marathon who was just a leisure walker. I gave her a few tips and asked her not to think and to just go for it. She diligently followed my advice, enjoyed the process, and completed the climb. She explained how my lessons on all these sporting events had helped to relate and transform her life, and strongly encouraged me to share the stories with people out there. All these made my heart sing.

These people have demonstrated how, starting off with self-doubt and hesitation which may just be like you and me when we start on something new or unknown, by taking the steps and advice, they had managed to overcome their problems.

I believe after reading to this point you may be wondering what is so special about me. Well, I always believe that everyone is born with a talent. You may acknowledge that wherever you are in life right now is not exactly where you want to be. I am not making promises that your dreams will come true or your problems will change, but I hope my experiences can help you deal with them in your very own special way.

In the pages that follow, I am going to share a range of real-life challenges – from getting myself out of a rut, plucking the courage to share something so personal between Richard and me, to overcoming the trauma of devastating family matters and illnesses.

As you read on, you will learn about the ways I keep myself moving. It may not turn out to be your way but I am sure that you will discover ways to reach your own "Iron Spirit", to recognise the weakest to the strongest parts of who you are, from one place of suffering to another of peace of mind, and to push through all the challenges and fears. You may or may not have discovered all the incredible powers you, in fact, already possess.

In the many years of life already lived, you have already come so far. Just look at your history, and you will see how much you have achieved in a certain amount of time. Then perhaps, you tried to set more goals in the same time frame, while all these planning may have overwhelmed you or made you give up many a time.

My intent is to put you back on the journey of life, learning and finding joy on your journey towards being the best you can be for us all.

GoGo Sof

Introduction

When the Door Opens

Skydiving, an experience in falling out from an airplane from a height of 4,200 metres, you pay a few hundred dollars for this, sign a waiver consisting of a thick stack of documents telling you how many people actually die, and they are not liable. You get nothing like life insurance or compensation of any sorts. Not even a single cent.

They go through a series of procedures like what to do at every height, how you should be jumping and even what to do to open the parachute on time.

No 100 percent guarantee.

You know that fear. That natural ingrained human fear of heights, the feeling of danger or even death.

Should I really do this?

Man's bucket list. Man's greatest dreams. Or so they say.

———◈———

I am not an adrenaline junkie. I am not a daredevil. The reasons why I jumped on the skydiving opportunity were the possibility of an unforgettable, life-altering inspirational experience and to probably kill my personal curiosity to see if it was as daunting as it seemed.

I had just completed our Gold Coast marathon, and I was buzzed with the need for adventure. But after making such a faraway trip of almost nine hours from Singapore in a foreign country, without much further thought, I thought why not?

After saying a yes, I wanted very much to kick myself in the butt the night before the dive to make a plane to go for this. I had done my research back in Singapore on the various skydiving opportunities and videos before this.

For the few days before the skydiving took place, Richard and I were stashed in the hotel in a quiet lane of Gold Coast, Australia. Not willing to pay for the chargeable internet connectivity, we did not make any phone calls or connect to our social media. We also did not buy any pay-per-view movies, which left us with the regular TV shows, and a few tourist brochures to keep ourselves busy. While Richard went through the brochures and maps, gave a rundown on what skydiving was all about and what to do in skydiving, I was bored. Whenever I took a chance and entered an unfamiliar zone or a new experience, I felt a sense of fear and what Richard would say about me – I would still do it.

The next day, we saw a couple of others who were joining us in this expedition. The van took us to Byron Bay, (a beachside town area in the far north eastern corner of the state of New South Wales, Australia, surrounded by lush rainforest, mountains and beautiful beaches) which was about two hours away. In the van, all we were talking about were our feelings to the jump, and all the free-flowing communication about our individual vacation leading us to this jump. It was a wonder how different people of different countries ended up here for the same purpose, as if they were just waiting to let out those wonderful "stuff" within them.

What about the twenty-page waiver document? They wanted me to sign on every single page. Without reading too much into it, I signed on every single piece. In two groups, we have undergone a briefing and several trials for a few hours. It was ridiculous; it was just a lot of information. I just wanted to do it now. As they demonstrated the various scenarios, the human ego in me was strong. I did not want to quit.

Not now.

Amidst the nervousness, we were taught to bend our whole body into a "V" shape at our pelvis area while pushing ourselves forward. It was a lot going on in terms of dynamics like turning, maneuvering, and landing. The airplane I took looked like a cheap scrap of metal to me, probably built during The Wright Brothers period before I was born. Did I really want to go into this small plane with about eight of us? No, I thought we would be suffocating in the plane before we had even jumped. Could this plane really go up that high? There were many what ifs.

The length of time going up to the diving location took about twenty minutes. But it felt like two years. I could not hold the excitement in me, while Richard started to get sweaty palms. This was the most nerve-wrecking part of skydiving. As the plane went higher, I was strangely calm. I was admiring how pretty the rivers and plains were.

For that moment, Richard was thinking of taking the shorter distance of 3,000 metres.

"You sure you want to do this? You will be the first one to go first then", replied one of the instructors.

Richard hesitated. He decided to join us all in going to the extreme of 4,200 metres up in the sky. They took us to 4,200 metres. *NOW* is the perfect time for opening the door to the power within.

While Richard hesitated in moving his legs, the professional skydiver moved him from behind and off they went.

Then it was my turn.

My professional skydiver told me that it was a little cloudy and the ride down could be a little windy and cold. I wasn't feeling nervous. But for the last few steps before leaning onto the edge of the plane, I realised this was actually happening. Before I could respond, he yelled, "Let's go!"

Before I knew it, we had jumped.

As instructed, I held my palms onto my chest and arched back. Anything that was sitting on my mind disintegrated. Maybe I had so much adrenaline. That feeling of free fall…it was zero gravity and no one was actually holding me….that feeling of being free. It freed me from any stress that had been occurring for quite a while now. This must be the reason that people who craved that rush of adrenaline that skydiving brings are called "adrenaline junkies".

In the midst of misty puffy clouds and noisy cold air brushing past my ears, I was staring at the thick layers of clouds as I descended at a speed of up to 190 kilometres per hour. With the pressure on the front of my body, my face froze in a grin. The loud air was rushing all around me.

I could see my skydiver busy taking photos and video of us. I was thousands of metres away from everyday buzz. I was flying and surrounded by the vast blue sky. Soon, I saw the airplane disappearing in the distance.

As I looked down, I was enjoying the view under the canopy thousands of metres above civilisation. I would have that feeling of stomach drop. No fear. No scream. Not even a sound. It was just simply not possible not to feel any awe. Those decades of seconds of floating in the air were just simply indescribable!

My eyes teared up and instantly dried up from the winds pushing against me. In less than a minute, my skydiver shouted, "Ready, set, go!"

Suffering from motion sickness, I was feeling nausea especially towards the end of the drop with the deployed parachute. The parachute opened. My body turned from a horizontal to vertical position. It then grew quieter. It took us about less than ten minutes as we snaked through the air with gushes of winds passing me. With the majestic and glistening lakes and greenery sights, I was actually enjoying this!

I then plummeted towards the ground soon after. We landed nice and soft with our legs lifted and our butts landed on the grass. It was simply that Top Gun character.

Pure mind. A feeling of accomplishment overwhelmed me. I was back to reality. Things started to balance out again.

Life is not going to be always you in search of the next adrenaline fix. It is about you savouring every minute every moment of it, touching your heart and finding your place here.

This is my leap of faith. Living life to the fullest is what skydiving was all about. The moment you leave the plane, you cast all your worries aside. It is just you and freefall, oh and probably a friend who is with you.

It is not easy to do that in every aspect of your life. There are great moments in life other than just screaming amidst the cumulus clouds of air and feeling millions and zillions of kilometres per hour.

Everything in life has something to offer. It may not be obvious to you. You have to look for it. It is there.

Perhaps less than five percent of the world population has ever skydived. And when I look back up at the sky now, I can gesture it and say, "I have been there. Have you?"

You just jumped out of an airplane, what can't you do now, Sof?

My skydiving experience in Byron Bay Australia gave me a strong faith in my infinite ability to achieve anything in life.

Part 1
Searching for the Strength of "I Can"

Chapter 1

The Power of the Dream

The tiled floor was filled with water, the bathroom floor drain was covered, and the room reeked of soap. I was sitting naked on the bathroom floor. There was silence. I cried and then wiped away my tears. For every tear I wiped away, it was a constant reminder of the difficult times I was going through.

I was breathing heavily, my chest felt tight and my guts felt knotted with nausea. This was the second time in a year I had sat down on the bathroom floor with a pair of scissors in my hand. My GCE "A" Levels were just months away and I had been struggling to get an "A" for every subject. My boyfriend had been helping me but my mum just did not like me spending my time with him. My dad urged me to stop seeing the guy to keep peace within the family. I cried uncontrollably as I slit a shallow line across my wrist. No one seemed to listen to me. I felt life was unfair to me. I had lost the spirit in me.

"Girl, where are you? What are you doing?" My mum was looking for me.

I thudded with my back pushed back to the wall, quivered, and felt on the verge of collapse. I was suddenly gasping for air in the enclosed bathroom. I threw the scissors aside. I looked up at the bathroom's ceiling, the white ceiling mottled with brown patches, that reminded me how messed up my life had been so far.

As my mum approached, I quickly put on my clothes, wiped away the blood stains on my wrists, held a towel around my wrist, and cleaned away my tears. I came out of the bathroom and made my way to my room, pretending I was studying. My mum came to me complaining about my dad being busy with his work and not listening to her about my grandma. All I did was sit still and listen to all her stories and complaints. What else could I say?

Nobody noticed what I had gone through for those few hours. My brother and my sister were in school. My dad was at work. I was not bothered by what anyone thought. I was still feeling something. Exhaustion mostly. Despair perhaps. I just wanted to get it over with – all these stories, all these complaints – just to lie down in my bed. I was nineteen.

———⋆⋆⋆———

I am a Chinese born in Singapore. Singapore, also known as the Red Dot, lies at the southern tip of Asia and Peninsular Malaysia. And it is not China. Singapore is a global city-state, known for being a global commerce, financial and transportation hub.

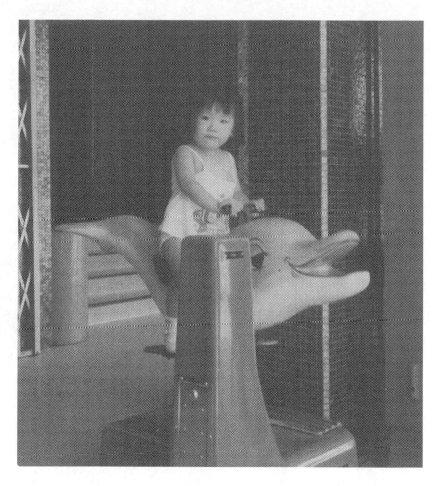

This was taken when I was two years old.

Growing up in a Chinese family, I had parents who were just like many others: they expected their children to be obedient and heed their advice wherever and whenever possible. I have one younger brother, and throughout those younger years, I remember that I could talk to him about anything. Whenever he did well in school, he was rewarded with the latest toys – classic MASK toys, hand-held games and game consoles. My younger sister, eleven years apart, arrived much later. All the attention shifted on my youngest sister, so I grew up pretty much on my own, taking care of my own school studies, homework and exams.

I could not recollect the times my dad had really talked to me, because even before I could talk to him about school, he had rushed off for his next workplace. So I no longer got too bothered about whether my dad really cared.

I had no possessions or any assets. At a young age, I had thoughts of living out on my own, but there was no way I could afford any room rental in Singapore. I was just a student, and I was forbidden by my mum to work. What was worse was that I possessed no sense of who I was or who I wanted to be. I was like a mindless machine, day in and out, studying and sleeping. This machine was breaking down. Lethargy overcame me. I just wanted to end the struggle.

Time in school was fun for me. My parents never taught me how to play sports or even games. I grew up having different interests in school – largely in sports. I was keen on learning the different sport games, so I always hung out with the different groups of friends. That being said, learning did not come easy to me.

The concept of winning a race came early. I was seven. I was nominated by my primary school teacher to participate in a novelty race in my school's Sports Day. Despite weighing heavier than most girls at that age, I was pedaling harder and faster than most of them on my training wheels. I wanted to *win*.

"Go! Go! Go!"

My classmates were cheering for me. I pushed hard, and we won fourth place that day. It was not a podium win, but it taught me the sense of achievement I could get from a race.

After the race, I continued cycling, went faster and fell on the uneven terrain. I was filled with fear! I expected a hard thrashing by my dad. But without hesitation, my mum rushed me to a traditional chinese medical clinic.

After waiting for more than thirty minutes in pain, one mid-fifties old man, cladded in white singlet and a pair of old slippers, slowly walked over with a bowl of dark coloured warm liquid and some ball-like pieces of cloth. My mum called him *shifu* (meaning Master in Chinese).

When *shifu* was trying to push the elbow joint back in place, I was hurting. On a scale of one to five, the pain was definitely a ten. I just shouted for him to finish up fast. The *shifu* rubbed my elbow with the cloth, and then wrapped up my arm in a bandage. I wasn't so thrilled about how bad my arm looked for a few weeks, especially all wrapped up.

My fear of my dad scolding me was unnecessary, when he came near me, he just sniggered and then walked away.

As I recalled my race, it was bloody hard out there. It was cool and I made every effort to win a prize. I raced on a bike which I had never done before in my life, and then falling down in pain. I accepted that, and a large part of me felt great for having a go.

Staying in a crowded city like Singapore, I did not have much acquaintance with the lakes or the beaches. I stayed in a self-contained four-room housing unit in a tall public housing flat with my family. The nearest swimming pool was at least five kilometres away. When I was ten, I remembered the anxiety in my mum as she felt I needed to pick up some swimming survival skills. Soon enough, she signed me up for swimming lessons.

I hated being in the water. I was the shortest in the class, with my chin just touching the water surface and feet barely touching the ground in a 1.5-metre deep pool. We were taught to kick water, swim freestyle, breaststroke and even backstroke consisting of a few minutes for each style, which to me felt like hours. I was never able to swim one complete lap without holding to the side of the pool. All I was looking forward to at the end of each class was the deep-fried fish balls snacks (ball-shaped patty made of pulverised fish) at the canteen.

In the final lesson, the coach told us that we would be undergoing a test to achieve the National Survival Swimming Award (NASSA) - Bronze Award. Here is what we needed to do - tuck jump entry from side of the pool and swim a good one lap of 50 metres, demonstrate "drown-proof" for one minute, tread water for three minutes, undress our pyjamas and make a float from the pyjamas, swim 400 metres, surface dive and swim submerged for at least five metres and finally, climb out from the deep end of the pool without the use of the steps. All these seemed to be too much for me.

With poor upper body strength and probably not getting the right strokes, I had difficulty trying to swim non-stop for fifteen minutes in the pool. Surprisingly, at the end of the class, I was awarded the Bronze certificate. I guessed the coach either did not want to have me as his student again or he simply could not be bothered over the actual results.

———◆———

After school, I would return home straight away. I would do my homework on the coffee table in the living room and watch the boys playing outside my window. There was one day when I got bored. I saw a boy cycling at the void deck of my apartment and excitedly went out, walked over to him and requested to have a try on his mountain bike, it was probably a few sizes bigger than me. It just felt so cool to be out on the road with these boys, after having watched them do their stuff for so long.

The ride started out fine. Then I started to go at a faster pace of probably about 15 kilometres per hour...20 kilometres per hour...25 kilometres per hour...I don't know. I just loved the breeze and the speed of the machine. So I went faster and faster.

As I was made one of the turns, the bike swerved. I fell hard and suffered a fracture on my left elbow. My mum was pretty used to me playing sports, falling down and fracturing myself throughout my junior years. I was also getting more familiar to my *shifu*.

It also seemed I had some sort of ankle instability. This was a condition characterised by a recurring "giving way" of the outer lateral side of my ankle. This resulted in skinning my shin and knees with repeated bruises and swells – falling and healing until scars were ingrained on my knees. And perhaps because of the numerous times I had fallen from bicycles resulting in repeated ankle sprains, that such "giving way" even occurs while I walk on a flat ground. Those scars from my fall have since carried to other areas of my life.

When I was in my early teens, unlike other girls, I enjoyed watching the boys play soccer. If I was lucky, I could even join them for a few rounds. During one of the games, I was rushing towards a ball with a few boys imminent on the sides. I took a big step onto the top of an iron grille that was covering the drain at the side. I slipped and fell.

This time, it felt more painful than usual. It certainly caused a huge scene. My teacher called my mum, my mum called my uncle, my uncle drove his taxi with my mum in his taxi, my uncle carried me onto the taxi and brought me to the *shifu* again.

"I am sorry. This is more serious than a sprain." The *shifu* described the lump on my ankle and touched it as I screamed.

He paused and then responded, "I think you need to send her to the hospital."

I was immediately sent to the hospital. The doctor operated on me, and put my leg on a huge cast. I suffered a slight crack on my right ankle. Those ugly looking sticks cost a bomb! In my head, I knew my dad was not going to be happy about this, having to incur these unnecessary expenses. After several falls, my dad had already warned me not to do any sports and to spend more time in my studies. I could not think of the consequences if I were to tell him that I fell while I was doing another sport! I was on crutches for a few months.

My dad has a temper. He can become abusive and verbal. All thanks to my dad's incessant putdowns, I never felt I could do anything right or even what he liked. With several jobs to balance at one time, my dad worked hard to feed the family. But I never felt he truly understood what I wanted – his time for us. I never really told anybody what was going on with my father. He had no friends, totally estranged himself from his relatives, effectively - no life. I was still making it look as if everything seemed okay to the world. His most effective weapon, which hurt the hearts of many, was his words.

———◈———

Sports soon became the proverbial elephant in the house, a topic that nobody wanted to broach. Being in a sports team in school was near impossible.

When I was fifteen, I picked table tennis as my co-curricular activity. I came home from school one day, excitedly ran towards my dad and told him that I had a school team selection the next day. My coach believed that I had an opportunity.

"Haha", my dad let out a disingenuous chuckle. "Remember to lose the first match!"

"You just don't believe in me making it in sports, don't you?" I shouted at my dad.

"No, I just don't believe that you can make it to anywhere with sports", my dad elaborated.

At that time, I really wanted to be in the school team. My friends and I had come a long way to reach that point after practising hard and with all that sweat during the weekly training sessions.

"Look at the best sportsmen. Where are they now?" my dad asked.

As an obliging teenager, I could not reply to that question. It came true enough, how much I had listened to my dad. I lost my first match. It hurt my pride. I felt I could not succeed in anything I did in life.

Being an average performing student taking eight subjects in school, I took after-school tuition classes. I did well enough to go into a school in a neighbourhood rather than a top well-known school in Singapore. My mum believed very much that my future would be a brighter one if I had been to a top school.

After six years in primary school, four years in secondary school, and two years in junior college, I actually preferred to go for a diploma in a polytechnic. After much fury and quarrels between my dad and I, my mum talked to me. My dad wanted me to go to the university.

Deep in my heart, there somehow still laid a magic spark. I never gave up trying to learn about sports and never stopped discussing about sports with my classmates. But I was in an environment where my mum kept reminding me to finish my university studies. She was right. School was all about studying, finishing homework, tuition work and assessment books, eating and sleeping. There wasn't much time for anything else.

———◆———

By the time I finished my college, I was eighteen, and I was weighing close to fifty-six kilograms at a height of 1.5 metres. I was overweight, wearing large or extra-large-sized school blouses.

I felt lucky to have met a boy named Andrew, three years my senior from a different school. Andrew was not the man of my dreams, but it seemed that losing him meant losing the only boy in the entire world who dared to go out with a fat girl like me.

My mum was not very supportive of my relationship with Andrew. She was superstitious as he was three years older than I was. She certainly carried a lot of preconceived notions. As a result of this, many disputes happened between us. Shortly after, Andrew left for his overseas studies in the United Kingdom and we lost contact with each other.

So, my entire educational plans and my life had been so dependent on what my parents wanted out of me. Indeed, the route to university was perhaps not my favourite choice but this was what was believed by my parents to be the passport to success in life.

Will the entry to university lead the path to my dream? I wonder.

Chapter 2

Finding A Place

The four years in the university was probably the toughest time I ever had. My dad wanted me to graduate with a specialised degree in Building and Estate Management. Just like him working in the construction sector, he very much wanted me to become a Quantity Surveyor.

I was a reserved student in the university. With up to six subjects per semester, I felt it was quite a handful to manage, and I did not join many activities. I did not like many of the topics in my course, and naturally did not do well in them. In some semesters where I had a choice of the subjects, I actually did well in subjects like Human Resource Management, Marketing and Management subjects. My second and third year results dwindled as my interest for the building subjects fell like stocks. By the time I reached my final year, all I wanted was to quickly graduate from the school.

As an undergraduate, I was still self-conscious in terms of my looks and figure. I wanted to have a boyfriend badly. Ranging from freshly squeezed lemon juices in the early morning, to fruit diets, slimming teas to pills to expensive treatments in the market, I had tried them all. When at movies, I did not even dare to touch the sweet or salted popcorns! My friends thought for a moment that I was fasting for a religious reason! After almost half a year of conscious dieting, it just did not make any sense that I was not losing much weight. I continued to starve myself, cutting out everything on the food I consume, and merely having just fruits for meals. Over those next few months, my weight fell. But I wanted to lose weight even faster, and ultimately turned to a starvation diet. I ate little and did a little walk home from my students' home. I was giving tuition to some students then. After finishing my classes, I walked home. Two kilometres.....three kilometres... I did not care how long those distances were. I also did not measure them. I just wanted to lose weight.

Well, I lost weight alright, probably my first biggest loss of eight kilograms ever in my life. At long last, my mum was sharing the joy of watching my kilos disappearing, and had the pleasure of shopping for new clothes which were a lot prettier, and definitely sexier on me. It led to an overhaul of my entire wardrobe along with my newfound confidence.

———◈———

Upon my graduation, I looked at my life. The new millennium dawned. I was full of hope. After years of studying, did I want to continue to study? Where was I supposed to go next?

Every classmate I knew applied for a related job in Building and Estate Management. But for me, I just could not bear the thought of counting the bricks and steel bars in a construction site for the rest of my life.

My confidence from the weight loss grew. I knew I could not shy away from the working world which I was about to enter. I deviated from what my dad wanted out of me and applied for a managerial position in a government agency. I landed my first job managing sixteen junior officers. As a leader, I was impartial and encouraged teamwork. These people were quietly working behind the operations, and serving the organisation for decades.

Trying to understand my dad now, I understood he must have been a man under immense pressure to feed a family of five, although plenty of which was self-induced. I would comfort myself each day at work that no matter how tough my job was, my dad's job was always tougher.

As the eldest in the family, I learnt to suppress my emotions, and aimed to be a good role model for my siblings. Little did I realise that I was emotionally wrecking myself with envy and with all the "whys", while pretending everything was fine. So for the first quarter of my life, I lived with what my parents had taught me, and I did what my parents wanted. And I related all these as being part of this concept of filial piety.

Now I needed to find my place out there.

Since childhood, I have always hoped to gain some freedom being away from home, and probably pursue what I like to do. I had a lot of excuses.

I really don't have the money.
My dad will be upset with me.
My mum will have no one to turn to when I am away.

Although all these were true to a certain extent, these were not strong reasons for my hesitation.

The moment I worked for about two years, I started thinking about living, and studying overseas. Working towards a Masters of Business Administration (MBA), I wanted the MBA as a goal just like how most high-flying working executives in Singapore had wanted. I wanted to acquire new skills and knowledge, constantly challenge myself with new practices and approaches, and push myself to continuously improve.

It soon grew from gaining of freedom to opening the door of opportunities with provision of new interactions and meeting people with great on-field experience. It could be a place where I could do what I really wanted.

I quickly looked at my bank account, and it showed I had less than S$30,000 on hand. This accounted for over twenty years of savings from childhood. I made a few calculations, and figured that all I could afford (barely) was an Australian MBA. It was a cheaper alternative than to do it in Europe or The United States. So I said to myself, "It will be enough." I had made my decision.

Since my dad has never supported me in any of my school activities, I never asked him for a single cent when I wanted to do my MBA. I just respected him as my dad, and told him my plans in studying overseas. His reaction was not surprising. It was only when I said I would be paying the school fees all by myself that he agreed with the idea.

I came to know about University of South Australia from my ex-boyfriend, Meng. Meng was a boy I dated when I first started working. I shared everything about Meng, and my relationships with a few other guys with my mum. My mum and I had arguments about him, and the same with the rest of the boys I went out with all the time, but this always ended in unresolved détente, so I kept engaging mid- to late twenties boyfriend bliss. So all these hanging out with my boyfriends, watching movies, feasting, going to the pubs, drinking and simply chatting made me feel as if I was heard and taken care of. And just like that, my dating days were over.

The opportunity to study in Adelaide, South Australia arrived soon after. There was this feeling that, for the first time in my life, I was competing on a global playing field to win that half-fee scholarship. Determined to do well for my MBA, I quit my job, took everything from my bank and went over. It sounded a little crazy. But I did it anyway.

Marketing, a well-established specialisation course in the university, was at the forefront and something where I could probably see myself enjoying in the years ahead. My biggest motivation was the opportunity to get back half of my fees through the scholarship if I was the top international student for the year.

Having that focus, everything I worked for in Adelaide were geared towards achieving an "A" grade, if not better. I networked, and worked in teams which gave me the best perspectives in terms of cultural mix and applications. During the midst of my course, I was running low on resources. I returned to Singapore, studied online while I tried to find a job and earn some money.

A vicious cycle set in once I returned to Singapore. With the ongoing events that were happening in my family, it was near impossible for me to study, work, and listen to my mum's woes all at the same time. I never really found a solution to balance all these, but just being there for my mum definitely helped me a little.

As I started to recall the tough times in my earlier school years, I wondered if the scholarship was really out of reach for me. Yet I never saw my years in studying Building and Real Estate as a waste of time. It was a valuable lesson for me to realise what I don't like and what I like. If I want something badly, I have to get it. No one is going to do that for me. I took up the responsibility of my own life, returned back to Adelaide, and finished up my course.

In Adelaide, I met various interesting people in different classes. And we did crazy things together, late night suppers, wine-tasting, driving down the Adelaide Hills in a convertible and chatting over a barbeque till morning. Although these seem like normal social activities one would do with one's friends, I felt like a child learning to walk as I began to do things which I never did way back in Singapore. I had my mum who was always worried I would get into some form of accident while travelling or having trouble with unfamiliar people. In Adelaide, the world opened to me. As I continued to venture out in Adelaide, I met different people and learnt about different lives.

In Australia, I did almost everything my mum did not want me to do.
I rented a car, drove up to the hills with friends, and stayed up late chatting
with friends.

Mei was a Human Resource Manager, and she came all the way from Malaysia to Adelaide to take an MBA specialising in Human Resource Management. Her husband had passed away from Leukemia a year ago and she had not been able to let go. What I saw in Mei was strength, and the healing process that was taking place.

Kay, another interesting Thai classmate, was the inspiration and the energy for all of us. Although a son of a huge family business and could easily live off his parents, he chose to carve his own path and set up his own business. His determination to take his own route to be different from his parents made an immediate impression on me.

Susanne, a German lady I knew from my Basic English class, was much taller than I was. She always looked cheerful and surprised whenever I shared something about Asia with her. Together with her then boyfriend, Christian, they sacrificed almost everything in Germany to come all the way to Adelaide just to start everything afresh. Talking about myself throwing in every dollar from my bank account, this couple had absolutely nothing and just travelled thousands of kilometres to Adelaide. I admired Christian's support standing next to Susanne right from day one. We might come from different countries of different cultures, but it never failed to show me the power of love.

To save money, I aimed to complete my course in two years, rather than the usual three years. I was the only one who squeezed in so many subjects within a single term. I just had to do it before all that feeling of whether I could do it came in. I was so focused in what I needed to do that I found every winter passing by quickly with all that studying and submitting of assignments, with the occasional coffee sessions with my friends.

I gave every assignment my all, and picked up lots of experience and tips of marketing trade along the way. I also developed an all-round positive mind and fitness, and connected the dots to most things that were happening around me. That versatility has served me well throughout the years. All of which led to the university selection towards end of the course for the recipient of the half-fee scholarship. This was a big thing in all respects - so the university's decision to select me, as an international student in winning the half-fee scholarship was a big honour. I felt that a dream coming true was just like a miracle. So much about the self-confidence I had also found within myself.

After the excitement of winning the scholarship, I came down to earth a little when I returned to Singapore. Personally, I was on a high, I could finally put the completion of an MBA on my resume. The scholarship was fine, but it was not a guarantee to a job.

It had been a long road, and since I had done my best, I just kept looking ahead. Eventually I found my best friend who somehow lit up a path towards what I wanted to do. That best friend was me.

Everything would be fine, wouldn't it?

Chapter 3

Seeking for Inspiration

While I watched my friends working with more years of experience when I was away in Australia, I felt frustrated. I was starting from scratch again in a new domain on my job. The ideal path to success that I was carrying with me in my mind was soon derailed by clashes with difficult people, even though they were not disastrous.

At work, I met bosses of all kinds in different organisations – manipulators, tyrants, aggressors, competitive, and control freaks, and even a suspicious wife of a tycoon of a multi-million dollar company. While my MBA prepared me in terms of strategic thinking, speaking eloquently and proposing answers even when I don't have the answers, it did not teach me to handle the people around me. Many a time, I asked myself if I could change the situation, put up with it, or just walk away. My conclusion was difficult people like them aren't going to change, just to make me feel better.

While working for an MNC, I saw what the life of a tycoon was like --- getting the best meals, personalised services at his beck and call, personal planes, and a stretch of houses that served the entire street. In Singapore, even at the entry level, a house would probably cost more than five million dollars!

That being said, I was given the opportunity of receiving a competitive salary package with a year of bonuses.

An entire year of bonuses, Sof…you could have retired early.

I worked til two in the morning, took a regular taxi home and reached office early the next morning. While I had colleagues suffering from chronic fatigue syndrome, I felt fat loaded with all the caffeine, muffins, burgers, and fries from the nearby McDonald's fast food restaurant. At the age of late twenties, I thought my life was totally taken cared of by working for this MNC but yet the next moment I realised that I could also be taking care of the potential health hazards that I might be facing.

So, for most of my earlier life as a young working adult, I worked as an administrative executive. I put in long hours at work, met up with my friends, and did what executives do: eat, drink, and complain about work and life. We talked a lot about things, issues, and dreams. We wondered and we talked, but we did not do much anything else. The idea of playing a game together with our friends was alluring. But the reality was, apparently, taking too much effort for all of us. The only real exercise we really did was to look for that pub which had suddenly moved!

When we stayed out late at night after work, we just could not understand why runners would wake up at three in the morning, and travel for about an hour, just to reach the starting line of a race. They then ran a 5-kilometre race, a 10-kilometre race, a full marathon, or whatever the distance, just to get a race pack consisting of a free singlet and a metal piece of no street value at the end of the event.

My MBA definitely did not teach me to do all these. It did not teach me to figure out at this moment in life, what I wanted to do, how I could find my passion, purpose or clarity on how I could change the world. It did teach me to see the big picture, and make calculated risks and sharp decisions. Moving on then was the healthy and productive option for me.

Perhaps, if I started to learn from others as to how they balanced their work and life while climbing the corporate ladder, or choosing a road less travelled, all these struggles with the same insecurities, frustrations, and life decisions would have knocked some sense into me. I was fortunate that I was still sane enough to make such a decision.

After my resignation, flashbacks of my former life returned: the kind of lifestyle which was not so cash rich, but was rich of smiles and laughter, the friends I used to hang out with, the freshly-brewed coffee that I used to drink as compared to those instant coffee, birthday parties, buddy meals, and night events that I used to attend were just so fulfilling.

I felt that the majority of our lives had spent almost 80 percent of our energy in school, just to aim to achieve that dream career. The challenge comes when our dear ones get less than 20 percent of that passion and energy. I tried new things, knowing what I want in a job, and feeling better about myself each time.

———◆———

Paving a well-trodden path to a better career was easier said than done. Yet I still wanted to be good at choosing paths for myself. With my planning, organisation development, and other transferable skills I had built up throughout my career, I then moved on to another learning organisation.

One day, a colleague came over to me, and asked me if I could take her position for a 10-kilometre corporate run. She had something on, and could not make it for the run. At that time, I did not know how long 10 kilometres was. Looking at how much she wanted me to take her place, I just agreed without any hesitation. As the race approached, anxiety was building up among my colleagues participating in the run.

They would train in the park behind the office every few days, while I was busy working behind my desk. I did not feel that there was a need to get excited with all the training and runs.

The race day soon approached. As I did not want to miss the race, I had set a total of five alarms on my mobile and my watch on the night before race day. I woke up at 5 am, washed up, had my breakfast, and travelled to the race site about two hours earlier. I queued diligently for my last visit to the toilet. By 8 am, I was ready at the start line. With all the excitement, I was visiting the toilet more often than usual. So I finally understood why people were waking up that early!

Holy cow! I am in this for real! I thought to myself. I was not so much worried about running, but I was overwhelmed with the thousands of people at the starting line!

"Good luck", shouted a colleague nearby.

Being new to the event, I stood way behind the starting line. I told myself not to stop running til I see the finishing line. I had no idea what was going to happen. The horn went off, and I started seeing the crowd in front of me moving off. Other than getting the nerves out of me, I was just eager to start running, and getting over the crowd quickly. My breathing became ragged as I felt like a donkey running a race with a horse. Soon, the anxiety to finish the race started to creep in. After the first kilometre, the crowd thinned out, and I breathed better. While running, I saw the first pack of Kenyans runners speeding across me.

Wow! They were really fast! I just started my run and have not even broken a single sweat!

After a few kilometres, I was approaching those lifesaving aid stations. Participants were spending their time hydrating, refilling their bottles with isotonic drinks, and scavenging for extra aid like ice and muscle rub. It then became a big traffic nightmare! Everyone was trying to grab a cup of that bit of energy, while I also needed to get my fluids in, while staying away from the bigger-sized men who were elbowing and trying to get theirs. Some runners fell while slipping over the thrown cups. Cautiously, I passed the distance markers one after another. I was also shocked with guys weeing up against trees, parked cars, statues, behind billboards – you name it, someone would be relieving themselves on it. I soon felt like an elephant stomping along the last three kilometres when my run slowed to a slow-moving jog.

Then before I even realised it, I saw supporters and families laying along the finishing line, and cheering for their loved ones. I finished my first 10 kilometres in an hour and a half. I would say this was not too bad a performance for someone who had not run since her school years.

Once you have crossed the finishing line, there was nothing like lining up to get your finisher medal that showed "Finisher for 10 km Standard Chartered Marathon 2005". Athletes were patiently queueing up in the line. Queuing up for a Christmas sale was not even close. Now, I understood why runners would sign up for a race and go at all cost to do the distance. While the gold medal was won by a Kenyan, this finisher medal meant a whole lot to me: I had already won my gold medal.

For me to run that distance with a fat piece of meat around my waist, I just felt it took me too much effort and energy. At that moment – and, to be honest, in many others – I was just happy to finish the grueling experience.

You could probably have guessed what happened the next day. While putting a strong front, I was feeling stiff, and I could feel the aches all over my body throughout the entire day. I sat on the toilet bowl with my quads screaming like overstretched rubber bands. I could not bend my knees or put on my pants to go to work. Stairs became my enemy for the day. I learnt to appreciate the elevator inventions of Otis, and took a longer time than usual to reach my office. I enjoyed the bling and glamour that came from receiving the finisher medal. Since young, I have always wanted to win a sport medal. Now this was close to it, and everyone was applauding me for the effort.

⸻⬥⸻

As I grew to my twenties, I tried to get established in a career, find a partner, and find my way through life. As I entered my early thirties, I realised that the dreams of my youth has slipped away, and that something like mid-life crisis was starting to stare at me right in the face.

I had stopped all my McDonald's meals, and had been trying hard not to gain any more weight. Yet I was still at least eight kilograms overweight. I was not fat, but I was still on the plump side. The only sport I did then was learning to play golf with my brother and his friends. Well, at least, I was getting some form of active lifestyle into my life.

One day, as I chanced upon a retail store, I was fascinated with this sport watch. It had all the powerful and cool functions – heart beat monitor, speed, pace, time trial, lap intervals, backlight, and many other functions. It was *the* Polar watch. This probably was the most branded and popular sports watch in the market then. I fantasised about how the different buttons on the watch could actually help me in my fitness program. I bought it. It was a hefty and ridiculous S$400 decision made, probably a quarter of my monthly wages.

Upon reaching home, I cast the watch aside. Just because I bought the watch, it did not mean I leapt out of bed the next day, eager to exercise, and use the watch immediately. I was still watching my TV, meeting up with friends, and spending my time with them. The watch was actually collecting dust in my cupboard.

I was watching a TV ad one evening. It was showing an upcoming Anlene branded Milk Powder Run that was happening in a few weeks' time.

"Could such an event actually exist?" I laughed. "I don't even drink that brand of milk!"

"How long is Dhoby Ghaut to Orchard Road?" I asked a colleague of mine.

"Relatively quite short", he replied.

I did not believe that such a race could actually exist along the busiest shopping belt in town in Singapore. It was a 1.6-kilometre run along Orchard Road. I thought to myself, if I could walk along the shopping belt, then I could definitely run the entire stretch too.

After figuring out how to get myself registered for the race, I found training for the race was the tougher part. I had no motivation to train. The only motivation I had was to make better use of my S$400 watch. That was a hell lot of money from my monthly income.

Days before the race day, I collected my race pack, and felt as amazing as everyone else in the race expo. I was ready for the race.

It was a Sunday. After a mass warm-up, the horn sounded. I had a quick glance on my watch and I started to run. Before I knew it, I had finished the race. I praised myself for completing the race. I was so happy that I forgot to stop my watch!

I had no idea what I was supposed to do with my watch, but it sure was a good experience and heartening to see so many female runners in a race. It did not matter if you were fat or fit. Every girl who completed the race received a gerbera, a finisher medal, and a bottle of water. We just got ourselves absorbed in a relaxed atmosphere with other runners. The air of positivity was just so strong! What a great way to spend a Sunday morning!

After the race, I told myself repeatedly to be comfortable and confident in my own skin. If an overweight 'elephant' like me who had not run since school years could finish a race, anyone could. I went back to office the next day, feeling proud to share with my colleagues that I had finished the race.

The rest is history.

Chapter 4

Trials and Turbulence

Near to the place where I lived, there was a canal of about 1.6 kilometres long. For years, I had been living near this canal; along it was this stretch of unused, secluded and fully sun-exposed road. Next on my list was jogging along this grueling stretch. Grueling as I termed it, because there was no shopping retail store to look at, or even a single soul to chat with.

How could I do any exercise in such an uninspiring environment?

Rummaging through my cupboard for running gear, all I could find was a tee-shirt, a pair of shorts, a pair of socks, and a pair of non-branded track shoes. For a start, I aimed to jog non-stop from one end to the other of this 'canal road'.

I tried, and I failed badly. My veins were actively squeezing out every blood cell I had, and my lungs almost ran out of breath. It was the greatest effort I had ever experienced. Not only did I lack the strength and energy, I did not have any fitness at all. I had no idea if what I was doing was right. I thought running was supposed to be just moving one leg in front and one leg to the back.

"Why is it that running seems so easy for other people?" I asked my brother.

He paused for a moment, and then replied, "First and foremost, go get a proper pair of running shoes. You can't be running in that pair of old track shoes."

My brother gave me a few tips: to control my breathing pace and not let my breathlessness control me. Taking his advice, I jogged slowly and reached the end of the canal without stopping. My heart was pumping fast, but I was not dying.

After the completion of that 1.6-kilometre run, I then set my aim to build up the distance. By the end of that week, I aimed to go for two loops, and I did. In this way, I was gradually increasing my mileage. With a goal in mind each time, I just kept going. After about a month, I was running about four kilometres. And three weeks after that, I joined my first 5-kilometre race. It then got longer and longer...5 kilometres...10...12...15...and soon 20 kilometres. My curiosity to know how far I could run kept me going. I grew so addicted to training for races that rain or shine, I would still put on my shoes and run. In fact, I loved running in the rain with my soaked shoes. Running then became my obsession!

Initially, it seemed frightening to run races of longer distances like 10 kilometres or more. To make the distance more palatable, I mixed up several 5-kilometre runs, with bursts of speed and comfortable runs, running and singing while I listened to my MP3. I set my goals according to my capability and confidence for the race, like being able to run a 5-kilometre race in six months or a 10- kilometre race in ten months, or even by regularly running a certain distance. Having the knowledge that I completed a 10-kilometre run before helped a lot especially during my struggles in my training runs.

After some time, I soon figured out how to make use of all the data in the Polar watch, and noted them in my log book. With the heart beat monitor on my chest synced with my watch, it was crucial not to run above my maximum heart rate. I enjoyed my runs going at a comfortable pace and ensuring that I did not get myself overheated.

For me, a race starts the moment I sign up. It is like a commitment made. I want to be healthy and ready. I will look at the race route, and eat what works best for my stomach. I do not even attempt to try any products at the race expo. I am not a lover for carbohydrates, so I often consume my good mix of carbohydrates from my rice or pasta together with my fats, proteins, and vegetables. While I run so often, I supplement my diet with multivitamins and glucosamine tablets. After every run, I also note how I feel and adjust my nutrition and recovery accordingly.

Running soon became a shopping affair, with friends updating about warehouse sales, and online sales. Being an extra-small size athlete, I often got a good buy at the race expo. And being an underpronator, I do not have too much trouble getting the right type of shoes. I usually buy a stability or neutral pair of training shoes of an older model at a lower price. So within a year, my cupboard had piled up with running singlets, finisher tees and several pairs of shoes. The sports attire outnumbered my working clothes. I was also spending less on my cosmetics, nail polish, accessories, and heels as my money went the way of my practical sports gears.

As an amateur runner, I heard about some of my running friends being tied down by their times, rushing through the races, and getting injured. They committed to a pace at all cost, went full speed ahead with goal pace, and ended up with a full blown crash and burn. Some trained with their friends and pushed one another, and got themselves injured by going for races they think their bodies were capable of doing. And some joined races for which they ended up not training for.

Derek Redmond, Great Britain's 400-metre runner, whose hamstring snapped during his event, went on to finish the race at the Barcelona

1992 Olympic Games. Hyvon Ngetich, an elite Kenyan marathon runner who was in the lead of the Austin Marathon collapsed 50 metres from the finish line. These athletes ran their bravest race, and finished what they started off. You may think this is bad luck, but it really isn't.

Without doubt, there are tons of reasons why running can lead to injury. I knew being too eager to increase my mileage and speed, while taking on new and greater challenges was not a good thing. I had to train smart, and set realistic goals to prevent injuring myself.

Because of the injuries that were happening to a number of my friends, it took me almost two years before I started my first half marathon race, and then eventually my first full marathon race. I took the attitude of letting them run their races, and I run mine. The most interesting fact was I did not know that the first full marathon race I had signed up for was happening at midnight!

⬥

As I trained for my full marathon, I took it nice and slow around my neighbourhood. The training included running a longer distance of more than 20 kilometres at a slower pace. To escape the hot blazing sun, I would wake up at four in the morning. This included running solitarily along long stretches of beaches without the aid of streetlights at times. These were the times I really searched myself, reminiscing about my life - how far it had brought me, and how much more I really wanted to go.

Running a long and slow distance can be a painful process as it requires patience and determination. I have an ex-colleague who stayed about eight kilometres away from me. Eight kilometres was a pretty good distance for me to run towards him and back. I would take out my mobile and started messaging him. With his red running top printed with the word, "pacer", well-worn Saucony shoes and shaved hairdo, Chris is a thin-looking athlete who understands my craziness, and excites me with all his speedy time splits. The stories he shares often keep my mind occupied as I continue my runs.

Elevations, turns, wind, and timing of aid station all affect split times. I admit running on hard roads can actually hammer our knees. On an average day, one can easily expend up to 20 percent of the fluids that support the cartilage around the knees and joints, and often I see people wait till they feel the pain running down their body before they get down to the problem.

Similarly, I had my own problems. My initial running experience soon revealed my weak gluteus medius and tight hip flexors. Without straightening my legs over the course of the strides, I was bending my knees too much, overstressing my quads with slow cadence, and disengaging my calves and gluteus medius. This was a sign of Gluteus Medius Syndrome.

As compared to the sports massage offered by professional sports therapists or sports clinics, I preferred visiting my "*shifu*" at my usual Tui Na (a traditional Chinese manipulative therapy) centre. This is not your typical massage you get from the massage parlours. Although this is often a cheaper alternative for me, the quality of his massage is never compromised. The *shifu* knows his stuff without having me to tell him about my problem. He recognises that I never have the habit of doing my warm-ups before my exercise. While I lie and face down on the treatment bed, he elbows and kneads around my glutes for about thirty minutes. By applying pressure on these meridians and nerves, he removes the blockages that prevent the free flow of qi, and restores the balance of qi in the body. It is often a painful process, but my body loosens up a lot more after the massage.

While I was doing well in my new running interest, I met up with some friends, and they often asked if I would still be running during my period.

"Why wouldn't I?" I asked. "Of course the feeling of running in a race with a soaked pad definitely made it worse."

While the sport allowed me to make more friends, in reality, my love life had not progressed much.

I was more tanned than before, I was getting more spots on my skin with the sustained sweating, and my skin was also peeling off from all the sun-burn.

Running did not guarantee me in looking hot. It was not that I did not have suitors. There was just something missing with the guys I was going out with.

What the heck! I didn't care about who was going to be my next boyfriend. I was concentrating on just enjoying my sport. Soon I found myself learning more about the sport.

———❦———

Everyone has his or her opportunities in life. At work, I was supposed to go to London with my CEO. However, at the last minute, my CEO decided to get another executive to go with him. Undoubtedly I felt disappointed, but I also felt relieved as this meant I had opportunities to do something else.

While I was drinking a cup of coffee with myself one day, I looked up and told myself that one day I would climb up that 73-floor Swissotel building. Chris had also shared with me about his experience running vertically up the Swissotel. It sounded challenging.

And here I was, in 2007, signed up, and was about to climb the Swissotel Vertical Marathon. Running vertically threw up different kinds of challenges as compared to our conventional races. Other than having to battle gravity, fatigue, cramped, stuffy stairways and protruding objects along the way, Chris advised to condition our body with several vertical runs.

And so I started to have a few training sessions with Chris. Chris was simply flying, while I was panting and pulling myself up the flight of stairs of an apartment block. Running against gravity increases the stress on our hearts and lungs, as well as musculoskeletal systems. The humidity and limited ventilation in the stairwell also makes our efforts tougher with the load on our hearts and lungs. Besides the training on the steps, I had my usual running, squats, and lunges to help build up some muscular power in my legs.

Come race day, I felt ready. It was my first attempt running vertically. Swissotel The Stamford building is 73-floors high, consisting of 1,336 steps to the top. The race start was different. Runners were tagged and released in batches every few minutes. My strategy was to run at almost 70 percent of my full pace efforts for as far as fifteen levels if possible, and then see if I could hang on there. I followed this strategy diligently. Most people ended up walking rest of the steps. The trick was not to set off too fast, and forget to keep some energy in reserve. With some momentum in pulling myself up every two steps at a certain pace, my breathing became harder, and my breathing was obviously getting louder amidst the climbing of the steps. I did not know the pace I was going. I just kept going, looked up at times on the floor number, and kept going.

On certain floors, we saw some tourists taking a peep at us poor suckers of oxygen, without doubt curious on what they were witnessing, whilst we tried to feed on the oxygen from the small, stuffy stairwell. At around the 40th floor, a second surge of adrenaline kicked in. But because of my short legs and with fatigue kicking in, I then began taking a single step at a time. I used every muscle of my quads, calves, and legs. Some runners stood aside to gasp some air, while some were sitting on the steps. I did not stop, not even at someone who was puking next to me. When the final floor seemed so near, I felt a burning sensation down my quads. This was the point where I could either stop to rest, or keep my legs going. I pushed myself harder, and I eventually made it to the top.

The view was so magnificent that it was worth the effort! I observed the numerous skyscrapers from a sedentary helipad position, taking in deep breaths, and taking in some water finally.

Thankfully we were taking the lift down. As I went down to 72nd floor to take the lift, I reckoned I better take a picture of myself. I was looking around for someone to help me.

Then there was this fair skinny-looking guy with a well-combed side-parting hairstyle who came over, and offered to help me. It did not really matter how he looked. I just needed someone to help me, and I was thankful he was there. His name was Richard. He was not a local as I discovered, yet looked like a pure local Chinese for which I was mistaken. We chatted a little as we waited for the lift and the results.

I guessed he wouldn't fit the bill of my mum's requirement. I thought to myself.

This was the photograph Richard took for me
on the 72nd floor of Swissotel The Stamford Building.
We then started to chat for hours after that.

My mum had many pre-occupied notions - must not marry a man from a foreign island, must not date a man from a certain dialect group, must not marry a man who is the eldest son in the family - the list just went on. All these criteria described Richard perfectly. Without doubt, every item on my mum's list was checked.

Oh my god! This cannot be happening. I talked to myself.

"What's wrong?" Richard asked.

"Nothing", I sheepishly replied.

Something came to my mind at that time. There were times to let things happen.

Today, I never have guessed I would have climbed that 73-floor building. There are times to make things happen. Now is the time.

At that moment, I was wondering why I had been heeding my mum's invalidated advice, and following her list of criteria looking for a lifelong partner for myself for so long. Something inside me initiated. It was definitely not the climb that got into me. This could be the guy who could make a difference to my mum and to my life. This was the moment I woke up, and started to live my own life.

I continued my chat with Richard. We were supposed to collect our manually-printed certificate after the race. Surprisingly, there was a bug in the system and this gave us a little more time to chat. A short chat soon after became a few-hour chat. Thereafter I offered him to come and support me in another upcoming race which he gladly agreed.

What did I just do? I hardly even know this guy!

Race after race I participated, I would also invite Richard to come along with me as I progressed. And together with me, Richard who was a short-distance runner, also started to run longer distances.

I guessed this was what "Going with the flow" really meant.

Chapter 5

My First Series of Marathons

When I was a child, I wished I could quickly grow up, and earn my own money. When I then became a working adult, I wish I could quickly climb up the corporate ladder of success, so that I could buy my very own possessions such as the latest mac book, phone, or even a car. The smallest new car you could find in Singapore could easily cost you S$80,000 or more.

Now that I had got to know this skinny-looking guy, it was natural that Richard and I started to date more often. However, somewhere along with my stresses, I started to pick fights. I also started to pull myself away from Richard. I felt nobody understood the situation I was in at work or at home. With all these running and the demands from it, life became a big confusion for me.

It soon came to a time in my career where I felt that if I did not get myself focused on other aspects of life other than work, I might crash one day. No matter how frustrated or angry I might be, those kilometres on the run which Richard and I had spent together helped to kiss my negative emotions goodbye.

As the day of the marathon approached, I carried no excitement or anticipation. The mark on my calendar shone brightly, as if I was going to have an exciting adventure to look forward to ... and so it did.

A marathon is a big thing. The event consisted of a pre-race carbo-loading party on top of its race pack collection. Being new to the marathon category, here at the party, I met all kinds of people – those who were here for the food and drink, those who were here to make friends, those for their personal reasons, and those who were ready to boast their number of completed races. Keeping myself cool from all the heat and excitement from the race, I went for the carbo-loading party, and then turned in early, and got myself prepared for the race.

My first marathon would start at midnight. I had my body clock adjusted a few hours earlier so that it felt like a morning run. I had no fear. I knew that no matter what, I would just keep moving forward. I was no runner. Neither did I have the thoughts of following the faster runners running below their 3-hour marathon pace. I just needed to make it to the 7-hour cut-off.

For me to remain calm before any race, it was crucial for me to arrive at the race site early for a carpark lot, go to the loo, and be mentally prepared. It was 10.30 pm. Cheers of anticipation roared over the entire race site.

At the stroke of midnight the horn went off. Typical at any race, thousands of runners packed the front of the field, and many runners were going at a fast pace of probably over 10 kilometres per hour. Just as any race, I was still holding a 500-millilitre bottle of water with me as I ran. Besides that, I was wearing a waist pouch, had two iced bottles, a few packets of energy gel, some kitkat chocolates, and a first-aid kit around my waist. No, I was not going for a picnic definitely.

As I was running my first two kilometres, perspiration rolled down my back. This was way earlier than I should be. As I neared the 5-kilometre mark, I slowed down. It was just the beginning of the marathon. I thought running in the night would be cooler. Amateur runners like me learnt that night temperatures had affected our effort and pace. With a marathon that started at midnight, not many runners were quite as well rested as they could have been. I was fortunate that I realised this earlier. I had an earlier lunch, and an earlier dinner, followed by a few hours of sleep. The first half of the race was humid and there was no wind. I ran at a pace where I could finish 10 kilometres in 1.5 hours.

As I ran towards the beach, I thought perhaps there might be some breeze. Unfortunately, there wasn't. It warmed up considerably during the second half of the race. So there I was going at an easy pace of 8 kilometres per hour. The plan was to take water and gel after the first 10 kilometres, and after every subsequent 5 kilometres. I was careful to avoid consuming too much water too early to prevent getting stitches. There was a risk of getting dehydrated too, so I poured all the water I was carrying on hand over my head and body. I ran past the beach, up the overhead bridges, across the void decks of apartment blocks, and across the granite grounds of the reservoir. By then I was soaked with perspiration and water and yet I was not feeling any cooler.

I went through the half marathon within 3 hours at a time of 2 hours 40 minutes, which was 10 minutes slower than my typical half marathon pace. After countless number of overhead bridges we climbed, my breathing became labored. I slowed down and I felt as if a 10-kilogram weight had been pounded onto my legs. I was still feeling okay at the 22-kilometre mark, but I just felt the need to walk to catch my breath back, and to prevent myself from cramping. I started to slow down to a few walks, but I tried not to let those walks halt me.

Don't stop. Keep going. I kept talking to myself.

I knew once I started walking, it would be hard to start running again. I tried to pick up the pace after a few steps.

The gel seemed to work. At each aid station, I also chose to take the isotonic drinks whenever available. After the 29-kilometre mark, it was just about moving my legs to cross the big 30-kilometre signage. I did not accept any gel at the aid stations provided by the event, as I could not get myself to swallow any more of the sweet sticky stuff down my throat. I decided to focus on my breathing. I breathed hard, and counted like for every 60 breaths, I would walk a few steps.

Along the entire final 10-kilometre stretch, it was a lonely road where you would dig yourself deep. You looked across the street, and all you see was the number of lamp posts you had run past. There was not a soul in sight.

Sof, why are you doing this when everyone is asleep?

I heard voices. It was just my mind playing tricks on me. I felt bored, but I had to remain focused. With 5 kilometres more to the 35-kilometre mark, I used my breathing technique to talk myself out of the pain.

Breathe, Sof, Breathe! Count the number of breaths. Control your breathing!

After I breathed in and out for about 60 times, I felt like a hog, tired, breathing heavily, and making awful breathing noises. After jogging for about 100 repetitions, I could not believe what I saw in front of me. The 36-kilometre signage was right in front of me. I looked at my running top, shorts and shoes. They were all wet, and were chafed in some areas. Now, it was all about me going all the way.

The last two kilometres felt like it would never end. By the 40-kilometre mark, my muscle cramps were starting to build up so intensely and insanely that there were not anything else left to do, except to jog especially slowly in a weird manner as I laughed at myself doing so. My toes started to cramp such that if I tried to reach my foot to rub it, my hamstrings would cramp up too. For months of reading about body form and muscles used for running, I just could not care now, and kept moving forward. It did not matter which muscles I had to use to get me to the finish line. As I saw the finish line, I sprinted my final 50 metres. I finished my first marathon in less than 6 hours. The happiest part was not about the timing, but the fact that I had actually finished a marathon.

After reaching the finish line, I was in a daze. I followed the crowd, and queued for my finisher tee and medal. I had a few friends who came over and congratulated me, but I could not remember who these people were. From that moment of pain, I actually stopped all my groaning, and realised that I had gained some form of power. It was definitely empowering to run this race together with these inspirational people.

"Now, what?" I wondered.

My abdominal muscles started cramping hard. I did not feel like sitting down either. I walked to my baggage deposit to collect my bag, chose a clean corner, and sat down. While some male runners get abrasion from their new running gears, I was basically getting cuts and abrasions from my sports bras.

That morning, I had a good, but painful shower. After all these long runs, cracked heels, hard skin, calloused toes, toenails turning black and falling off, I had not imagined myself ever chafed that much. Under the humidity of the weather, I suffered blisters and toes that got rubbed, and heels with nasty-looking cuts. After that, I also had my best breakfast ever. This was one marathon I would never forget in my life. At that moment, I felt I had wallowed myself in my own misery for too long a time.

I was running along a quiet stretch of road in Sundown Marathon 2009. Richard, who was carrying a bag of drinks for me, joined me in the run subsequently.

Running had become a large part of me such that it had rechanneled my energy. Other than the sheer enjoyment, the freedom, and health benefits I had gained, these races had enabled me to count more blessings than the bruises. I was starting to know the industry better, and I was seeing how people were driven by their achievements.

I was carrying the torch in Peace Run (formerly known as World Harmony Run) which was a global torch relay to strengthen international friendship by passing the torch over 100 nations around the world.

Things happened for a reason. Amidst all the work and home matters that were happening to me, I took a step back, and realised that I had to control whatever I could, to love myself, and to rise above all challenges. I often hear the statement, "Life is ten percent what happens to you, and ninety percent is how you react to it." It remains true till today.

With shared goals and perspectives set from some of these past races, Richard and I came back together. It had been me all along, who thought I was not good enough for him. Since then, we did not look back, and moved forward instead.

As a dedicated runner with ambitious goals of running marathons on the other side of the world like The United States or Europe, I recognised that continuously participating in local races in Singapore could be a costly affair. In order for me to save up enough money for an overseas race experience, I chose to run in charity races, club races, and smaller races which were easier on my pockets.

The year 2009 was a year I tried several new races. This year was also a period where minimalist shoes just started to flood into the Singapore market. Little was heard about barefoot running in Singapore then. While there was a sudden craze of people changing their footwear to such minimalist shoes, as they believed these minimalist shoes could help them to run better, I saw no reason for me to change my shoes.

At one of the mornings, I shared with Chris about an upcoming "Bare your Sole" race. This was my first attempt in a barefoot run.

I heard how the runners were discouraging one another over the kind of terrain we had to run. The tarmac ground was not totally smooth, and the pavements were neither gravel-free. Around the parks, I could see leaves all over the place.

As we took off our footwear, and got ourselves standing by the starting line, I told myself this would be a test of pain threshold.

When the race started, I could see the discomfort in some of the runners. I too felt the little stones and all on the ground, but I kept going. As I closed the gap on the top five ladies in front, I took a quick glance and all of them looked younger than me.

I did not look back after that. It just meant I had to work harder than anyone of them. I kept surging and pushing myself, and ran my hearts out to finish the race. It was only then that I felt a pain on the skin of my soles. I had bared my soul with huge blisters on my toes and soles of my feet. I slowly limped to the medics as they bandaged my soles up with some gauze.

As I was chatting with a fellow runner friend about how tough the race was, Chris overhead an announcement.

"In third place, we have Sof.....!"

Chris shouted for me. We paused for that moment, and listened to the name being called again. We wanted to avoid any embarrassment. And then this time, it was real.

I was so thrilled! Never in my life have I imagined myself winning anything in sports. The fat old me was no longer around.

That prize meant so much to me. This was one race where all runners stood on the same ground with no shoes, and all runners started from ground zero. There was no Nike, no Asics or any branded footwear apparel to help us.

From top half of thousands of runners, to top one hundred of the runners, I soon found myself moving up the position races after races. The "Bare Your Sole" race remained a moment of which I stayed true to my goals, and made me commit to what I started off.

The word of "cannot" which I had heard all my life from my dad had suddenly become "can" for me.

————◈————

After joining numerous local races, I started looking for races outside Singapore. I discovered the joy of travelling and racing. My preference for travelling overseas had always been for leisure rather than for racing purposes alone. However, as time passed by, it has become a fine line between the two.

As compared to the races in Australia or in The United States with seasonal weather, the races in Asia are largely hot and dry, or hot and humid. Before travelling, I always carry a checklist to ensure all items are in place. When I reached my destination, it is always very tempting to go shopping, or just walking around a new place. As much as I usually take it easy for any races, Richard is always there to constantly remind me to get sufficient rest before a race.

Because of the proximity of these Asian races, the international crowd consisted of mostly Japanese, Singaporean, Hong Kongers, and other South East Asian Countries. With a quick glance at these runners, I could see them doing their warm-ups in groups among their own communities. Some of the elite runners seemed to be floating and gliding through the air as they jogged around the starting line. Without doubt, these Asian runners seemed to be committed to run, and committed to run well.

While there were similarities in terms of flatness for some parts of the terrains in Thailand, as compared to those in Australia like Gold Coast or Sydney, races like Bangkok Marathon demonstrated its challenges from the humidity and the pollution. While the roads were not entirely closed to traffic, runners seized the opportunity to enjoy some of the grandeur and scenery in terms of the starting point, and the journey to the finish. In Bangkok Marathon, we ran past the Royal Grand Palace with the Thai Bands, across the Rama Eight Bridge, and past the Thai Imperial Guards. In Phuket Marathon, I enjoyed the clear coastal sea, and serenity of the villages, while running under the hot sun. Though these races started way before sunrise with a cool and temperate weather, the trecherous heat got to the runners midway through the races.

Terrains for races in Malaysia and Thailand are also well-known to be hilly. Being a slow runner, I was prepared for the aid stations to run out of water by the time I reached them. These aid stations were often undermanned while most runners were patient enough as they waited for their water. At every aid station, I could see people pouring cups of water down their heads. With the amount of water I was carrying along in the several bottles in my pouch, they were fully utilised throughout the races.

I was running the Phuket Marathon under the hot sun, and I had
sponges soaked with water placed under my sports bra.

However, whenever aid stations were available, there were plenty of fruits like watermelon and bananas to choose from. As the sun rose, the temperature increased, and the environment grew real hot and humid. Traffic in some of these countries like Thailand, Cambodia and Malaysia were quite heavy, so this explained the pollution. I was also prepared to struggle through the mess quite a bit in the last 5 kilometres. It was absolutely delightful to receive food and beverages from sponsors like McDonald's and Milo at races like Bangkok and Malaysia at the finishing line.

As Richard and I grew in our journey of marathons, we analysed and discussed about the race events as a whole. Value-for-money was important to us. We had grown beyond just getting a finisher medal or a finisher tee. It was the holistic experience we were looking forward to.

While marathons in different countries could be organised differently, runners expected the second half of the marathon to be tougher, as the body got tired. After mid-way point, difficult as it seemed, I tried to speed up. This was where it was getting tougher! Some pacers were dropping off their pace like dead flies, while some pacers had to let go of their balloons.

Questions crept in – training volume, dietary concerns and for some, even self-doubt. There was no time for regret. When I was focused in making use of all the right opportunities laid out in front of me, all I did was to just keep going at it.

I was seriously tired in the last few kilometres, but to ensure a Personal Best, I drove myself to keep going. As we approached the finish line, I displayed my usual strong sprint, overtaking one or two runners. It was a good feeling to finish strong. As I looked at the clock near the finishing line, I knew I could finish below 5 hours, and in fact may be able to finish with a nice number. I achieved my Personal Best for Gold Coast Marathon with a time of 4 hours 44 minutes.

In life, the reality is that I will have great days, and I will have tough days, but how I approach those days is entirely up to me. The choice I make is for me, not my mum nor my dad. Everyone has a choice. You have a choice too. If I have heeded my dad's advice such that there is no future in sports, I will never be able to stand at the podium, or see the wonderful people and culture around the world.

Under the cool weather, I went for my signature finish at Gold Coast Marathon 2009.

Chapter 6

Looking for The World Championship

After consistently running for about two to three years, I completed running races of various distances – 5 kilometres, 10 kilometres, 15 kilometres, several half marathons and marathons. I treated every race as a part of training. So what? Who really cared about whether I had finished a marathon? When I went for job interviews, not many out there knew what a marathon was, or even appreciated the spirit that went into the completion of a marathon.

All of us undergo one same event, that is, our life. We all want to do our best, and achieve our personal best. We do everything possible to make the best choice at any point in our life, based on the resources we have, and the thinking we consume.

After my experience in running a midnight marathon, I sought around for experiences shared by marathoners who had raced in both hot and cold countries. I had different people who gave different pieces of advice.

How did I pick and apply the right advice given by someone with whom I thought, or I knew could possibly make a sound judgement?

The answer I have found throughout the years and talking to people of all ages, was that it is all within myself. Before we could pick up any advice, with the common cup analogy, we must first be willing to "empty the cup", and drop all baggage, ideas, and thoughts we have. With an open mind, we will then allow new ideas to come in. I have so often heard of people making such comments.

"Yes. I am being open. I am willing to listen."

There are two types of people. Those who validate whether they are open to the idea with questions on validating their actions based on past or preconceived notion, and without making peace with their past. Then there are also those who ask forthcoming questions to get to their end-goal of what they want to be or where they want to be, without bringing up the past. All the examples or stories shared by people who have completed or win the races did not mean they would all apply to me. It is always easy to allow our emotions cloud our judgment, and make impulsive decisions.

Everyone has a dream, and everyone has a goal. But what is the plan? Often before the races, I had heard from participants who said that they would just go and run the race. And when they could not run anymore, they would just walk the race. And surprisingly, there had been stories of people who did that and they too had run a good race time.

This could be a plan. Everyone is different. I am only 1.55-metre tall, with short legs and possibly still carrying body fats of up to 30 percent. I cannot just go to a race and give all my energy in my first half of a race.

When I first started my plan, I read about training techniques in running magazines. Paula Radcliffe, a Great Britain woman marathoner ran a record of 2 hours 15 minutes 25 seconds. With an awkward running gait, she ran marathons based on feel and "no limits". Carl Lewis, one of the great runners in the twentieth century with nine Olympic gold medals and eight World Championship gold medals, had unparalleled skills in long jumps and sprints. His success stemmed from his good and almost flawless form, shifting his support from his hands to his feet as he gained momentum and speed.

Inspired by these runners, I often faced myself with the mirror by my side, trying to remember the pose and angle. It seemed either I had a mobility or a flexibility issue, not surprising to me especially I had umpteen times of spraining my body parts when I was young.

Chris is a faster runner than me. Between Chris and myself, we contended over sex difference between men and women, between the body shape, heart size and lung capacity and so on between Asian and non-Asian runners, and Kenyan and non-Asian runners. We discussed about theories in the ways our ankles dealt with the toeing off part of our strides to varying rotations in our upper bodies. We even showed one another over the posture, leaning angle, foot placement, mid- or front- or heel-striking, arm swing and stride rate, and yet maintaining a strong core with an upright spine. There is a lot of biomechanics going on. Running is the simplest yet the most complex of the movements done under the full load of gravity.

Three years after I ran my first marathon, I aimed to better my timing for the same marathon I first joined. Perhaps this was what you so-called chasing after a Personal Best. That year, in 2010, Sundown Marathon was held at midnight again. And I was determined to do better than my last.

I set out my plan, which was to diligently use the spreadsheet, schedule all my training sessions, eat well, train well, sleep well, and go for the race. I was following the "best advice in running" and any other available sources of advice in training for a marathon. With up to four months to train, I aimed to do a personal best with training sessions ranging from running 5 to 8 kilometres per day, stretching up to 10 to 15 kilometres per day, doing the longer runs of up to 35 kilometres during the weekends, and a tapering before the race. That sounded like quite a *BIG* plan.

As I aged, my body started to get a little lactose intolerant. Though it was not common, I had a few occurrences with breathing difficulties. I rushed to the toilet, had loose bowels, gasped for air, and sat at a well-ventilated area. One of the doctors suspected that it could be on-the-go gastrointestinal issues and irritable bowel syndrome. All cheese and milk products on pizzas, pasta and coffee did not go well in me. As a result, I only ate a piece of bread spread with peanut butter, and a cup of honeyed water for breakfast before a race.

That year, the hot humid race started 30 minutes after midnight. I was running at a good pace til my first 10 kilometres, which was within 1 hour 15 minutes. At the 15-kilometre mark, my breathing became heavier. I could not understand why. I just proceeded. I was now aiming to reach the half way 21-kilometre mark. At the 18-kilometre mark, I started to feel an ache on my stomach.

No! Not now!

I desperately needed to go, and rushed for the nearby toilet along the beach.

Dripped down in sweat, I sat on the toilet bowl, wondering what was wrong with me. I was having cold sweat. When I was ready to stand, I had another stomachache.

I spent a lengthy 15 minutes in the toilet. After coming out, I aimed to run til the 21-kilometre mark. By the time I had reached the halfway point, I had already run to the toilet twice. This was not the day it meant to be. I had practised this distance over and over again. It never happened like this.

At mid-point, I asked myself whether I would like to stop and to go back as all my baggage were at the race start, or to walk back to my home which was about 6 kilometres away. If I were to walk home, I would have walked towards the finish line. I sounded really silly to walk back 21 kilometres when I should be going forward. Disappointed with my worst ever performance, I moved forward. More and more runners were running past me. At the 25-kilometre mark, I went to the toilet again. After my exit, I saw Richard behind me.

"Eh? Why are you here? You should be ahead!" he exclaimed.

I explained I had stomachache issues. Richard decided to accompany me as we walked. At about 30 kilometres, I was already demoralised. I knew that after the 30-kilometre mark, I would have difficulty looking for a toilet. I popped in some medication and continued. By the time we reached the 35-kilometre mark, I told him "Let's run to finish line." And I picked up the pace. Richard was left behind.

As I saw the finishing line, I cried. They were tears of all my efforts down the drain.

That was my most painful last 5 kilometres to the finish line. All the planning and scheduling, all the hard work, all the training were all gone caused by this unknown stomachache issue. I started to ask myself if I had consumed anything unusual. I had my usual meals, hydration and nutrition.

No matter how much preparation I had done beforehand, sometimes on race-day, things like this just do not go to plan. Such a disappointing performance could have left a void of all motivation for me to continue. However, when I look back at all the marathons I had run, I was still running well, and injury-free.

Realism hit me. It led me not to be overly optimistic about planning my marathon race pace or finish time target. Had I not listened to my body and slowed the pace, I could have suffered dehydration, heat stroke or any form of unconsciousness. I counted my blessings that I could still finish the marathon.

❖

Just as any typical avid runner, reading the Runner's Magazine was a norm. As a runner from a country like Singapore, it never failed to surprised me with the numerous fun races in the United States. One day, while I was flipping the magazine, there was one particular race that amazed me. It was the Walt Disney Goofy Challenge Back-to-Back Marathon – half marathon on the first day, followed by a full marathon on the next day.

Is this for real? It was like a childhood dream come true. It sounded crazy, but when I set my eyes on those beautifully crafted finisher medals, I was determined to complete this race. I signed up for the race and trained for it.

December 31, 2010 was the last day of the year. Just two weeks before leaving for The States for the Walt Disney race, I was feeling excited and dated my mum out for lunch. After a heavy lunch, she was driving me home. I felt so comfortable sleeping at the passenger seat at the front of the car.

Then calamity struck.

My mum dozed off while she was at the wheel on the highway. Before we could react, the car had hit the concrete barricades lining the side of the highway. Fumes emerged from the front of the car. The safety airbags of the car were fully inflated. It was just like the scene of an accident in the movies. I was half-awaken. The next thing I knew, I could hardly move. There was no pain but I just could not move at all. I thought for a moment, my body could be in a wreck.

I opened the car door, and waved my hand out for help. A man came by and carried me to the side of the car sitting by the road. He asked if I was alright. There was no blood, no fracture, no broken bones. But there was definitely shock and numbness in my legs. For that moment, I was worried that I might not be able to go for my Walt Disney race anymore. I could not remember whom, but I remembered someone bringing us to the doctor, as my mum and I suffered bruises and whiplash. The doctor comforted me that I would be ready for the race by then. We were lucky we had our lives back. As for the car, the front of the car was all gone.

These were pictures I took while I was sitting on the side of the road and was unable to move my legs.

My memories following the release from the various visits to the doctor are a catalogue of small victories: trying to walk for a few hundred meters carrying all the bruises in my body on the first few days, doing yoga poses with all the aches, running my first 10 kilometres for almost 90 minutes.

I repaired myself bit by bit. Every day, I got up and pushed my body. Without doubt, the pain of the bruises was all there. Every time the pain came, I asked myself if I would like the accident to beat me. One week before a big race, there was definitely frustration. But it seemed to be the same mental battle I had to shake off me.

Running in Asia versus running in The States are totally different scenarios - one of the differences being the weather. The weather in Florida then was just perfectly cold for me as compared to the heat in Asia!

I had Richard going with me for this race. Running in Disneyland was an enjoyable one – beautiful street, mighty castles, handsome princes and pretty princesses and the countless number of characters that lay out on the street. All these would have taken any stress out from us. Having learnt our lessons from our past trips, we stayed in an accommodation which was near the starting or finishing point so that we did not need to limp back painfully after the races. We enjoyed ourselves at the race expo - collecting the colourful race pack, looking through in detail the wide range of brands of exhibits and sale items.

On the day of the half marathon, the weather was freaking cold. It was about 5 degree Celsius. We prepared bottles of hot water, and held them in our gloves against our faces. Despite having old unwanted clothes to cover our faces, Richard was feeling so cold he had to wrap his ears with his clothes. We regretted not paying for the VIP tentage, which would have provided warmth to us and on top of the Disney characters we probably would have got to take photographs with. As the starting time approached, the weather turned colder. Near the starting line, there were hailstones!

Finishing the half marathon was easy. The key was not to go 100 percent, but to reserve some energy for the next day. We returned back to our hotel, and ensured that we had a good rest for the next day.

Running a race within Disneyland was one of
the best things ever happened to me.

On the day of the marathon, it was still a cold morning. We very much appreciated the VIP tentage we paid for this time and enjoyed every single minute of it. Richard was starting to feel some strain on his ITB, which stands for Illiotibial Band, or simply lateral knee pain. He told me to go ahead if he could not go on.

The marathon started, and Richard had already started to walk due to the strain he had on his right leg. At about 10 kilometres, I went ahead. This time round, there were more Disney characters and for that moment, I felt like a child freed from all troubles. The voices of

Cinderella and her Prince, the songs of Winnie the Pooh, the long nose of Pinocchio - all these were my childhood friends whom I recognised.

At about 28-kilometre mark, I slowed down to a walk, and took some pictures with the Disney characters. The pain at this point was all dissolved with the different Disney characters I saw along the way. At any point, I just could not see Richard. I took my time to embrace the atmosphere with Mickey Mouse and Donald Duck at the finishing line. For this fifth Walt Disney Goofy Challenge back-to-back Marathon, I bagged a total of three heavy weight medals - a half-marathon Donald Duck finisher medal, a full marathon Mickey Mouse finisher medal, and an additional Goofy Challenge finisher medal. And these medals were huge!

After I completed the marathon, I walked over to the VIP tentage and tracked Richard's race. It stopped at the 27-kilometre mark. I was getting a little worried. I waited. And waited. It was already 7 hours, and the cut-off time was 7 hours.

Shortly after, I saw Richard limping forward. He had made it. He was gritting his teeth. I helped him to the chair in the VIP tentage, and brought him hot soup. He sat down in pain, without speaking a single word. After a rest, Richard said he could see the sweeper truck at the other side of the lane, and he was running away from it. As we talked about the race, we rested while he could not move for hours. Everyone was packing up, including the tentage, the buses and all. He was still in pain - a happy one. He can never forget what he had gone through. Fortunately there was a cart, which came along and kindly sent us back to our hotel.

This race was unforgettable because we had seen how badly when a human being wanted a certain thing, how much one would work for it. While running became a larger part of my life, I admitted I was not a prodigy in running.

Now, I had been to the happiest place on earth, what's next?

A mental fortitude drives us forward in life. This is what I called The World Championship approach. To succeed, we all need to make the best out of every situation, put in the hard work, take the extra time needed to realise our aspirations. There is no plan B. Plan B sucks. There isn't going to be another fifth Walt Disney Goofy Challenge Marathon.

In the process, adversity will strike, and we make our plans, take disciplined action to make solid changes to our lives, learn and grow from them.

Whether you think you are just another typical performer, an athlete, a worker, a parent or a peak performer, life will begin and will end with your state of your mind. Richard and I are from Asia, and continually go towards the other parts of the World just to complete daunting races, which we had never done in our lives. We went, we fought, and we succeeded. After we have participated several half and full marathons locally, in Asia, in Australia and in the United States, a large part of our journey involved listening to stories of runners of various states.

We all deserve to shine and be successful. But we can only achieve this by embracing any opportunities, and going for the World Championship. The Iron Spirit is within us all, which allows us to work to achieve superior performance, and gives us the best shot for personal greatness.

———◆———

Chapter 7

Going beyond the Distance

Back in Singapore, there seemed to be a rise in the number of endurance sports and races. There was a sudden increase in women participation in these sports. An ex-colleague shared with me the idea of training in a gym. I hesitated joining a gym to get access to some sort of motivation. I was already paying for race fees, trips and never-ending list of sport accessories. I just could not justify paying for a S$80 monthly gym access if I were using it only once a week or even once a month. I definitely need the much sought after coffee I deserve after every long run.

Structuring my training around my working hours was not easy. I eventually signed up for a gym which was near my office at a low membership fee, wore my sports bra or swim wear under my work clothes to make a faster transition from work to exercise during my lunch hour. Sacrificing a high calorie-laden lunch with a healthier option several days a week could now be made possible!

At work, while I tried to clear the stacked piles of unread documents and emails, I developed a team who were initiative and progressively doing well in their delivery. I had one particular colleague in my team who kept me focused on the sport, motivated and applied whatever I learnt in the sport to work. On a bad day at work, she advised me to pull the weights in the gym or drench myself in the sweat amidst my run and ride. I was just blessed with such opportunities which allowed me to think through some of my work before reacting to them.

At the gym, I regularly see women talking among themselves trying to lose weight for races and athletes being obsessed with nutritional needs. That sounds good but it will not be very helpful when they are racing and need to assess carbs for fast, high-intensity fuel and their body have none. Women also risk losing their menstrual cycle and as a result jeopardising their long-term bone health.

With regular replenishment of supplements like glucosamine, magnesium, iron and vitamin C, I was concerned with taking enough energy with the rise of energy expenditure so that my recovery, thermo regulation and reproductive function were still performing well. Singapore's reputation is a food paradise with tantalising cuisines such as Chinese, Indian, Malay to international cuisine. My biggest challenge was not having no food to eat. Rather it was having the luxury of choosing what, where and when to eat. I eat like an athlete – sandwiches, salads, wraps and soup noodles and snacks like nuts, fruits and cereal bars. I ensured my training revolved around my dining choices and worked hard to earn the meal I deserved.

After running in the parks and roads for some time, I raised the bar by hitting the trails. Trail running is a different ball game.

Located conveniently and centrally in Singapore, MacRitchie Reservoir has always been a familiar cross-country race haunt since my secondary school days. It probably still is the only location where I can escape inhaling exhaust, breathing in deeply the humid, forest air and get a good sweat out once a week. Because of the undulating terrain, running through the trails, pavements and boardwalks of the reservoir is never a pleasure with the grass, gravels, tarmac and loose soil beneath your feet, not least climbing up and running down the gradients and sometimes slipping off them too.

Eggs Benedict. Pancakes. And a good cup of latte. These were the motivations that drive runners on the other training routes past Orchard road, up the Dempsey Hills, past the Botanical Gardens. With certain shorter races passing through some of the hilly routes of varying inclinations, we had been challenged with killer hills, muddy trail runs, flights of stairs and loops of compact forested areas. From long gradual hills to short steep ones, our runs had rewarded us with scenic canopy walks and breathtaking water and green views. At other times, Chris and I would probably be interested in the cheaper alternative of prata (a fried fluffy and flaky flour-based crispy pancake that is cooked over a flat grill) meeting the meat-based curry gravy drenched down with a cup of tea to set us back on a chill mood after a good run.

This was a trail-running race held at Tampines Mountain Bike Park and Trail Singapore (now defunct).

With popular trail races like The North Face which take runners through the forested areas and slopes of MacRitchie Reservoir, Bukit Timah and Mandai, I signed up for the 25-kilometre The North Face race. I gave little attention to who's who in the ultra running scene.

In a pre-race event, I attended a workshop introducing Kilian Jornet. As a humble, talented and an extremist athlete, Kilian remained unbeatable running 1 to 320 kilometres over unique hills and grounds. I watched in amazement on the ultra running scene with ubiquitous enthusiasm and energy of these runners, coupled with incredible uphill or downhill speed over the roughest terrain. It took a certain amount of guts and definitely some madness, edged with some alpine and gradient proficiency to keep oneself safe in the mountains. And here we were talking about mountains and not hills. These ultra-runners were simply crazy. Who would have imagined the inspirations from these runners had laced up our Asia runners and set the recent brew of the trail running revolution?

Running a trail race like The North Face looked pretty much the same, going to race site early, checking in our gear and undergoing a mandatory weighing of our hydration and race supplies. Here, I saw less familiar faces. These were the faces of the ultramarathon runners from countries like Malaysia, Thailand and Hong Kong.

Hong Kong trails, like those of Lantau, Pak Tam Chung areas, well known for its terrain and scenery as varied as its city contain the most challenging undulating terrain of forests, shrubs, creeks, reservoirs and big hills of over 760 metres of serious elevation. Thailand mountain trails, like those of Chiang Mai and Bangkok, include a tropical rainforest run with uneven terrains, rocks, trenches, and steep parts with 500-metre gain over three kilometres and gradual elevation gains over longer distances. Athletes also run through the greenery and magnificence of the paddy fields, buffaloes and breathtaking views on long lakes. These trail runs are more than these runners' high after completing these long distances. The biggest barriers were often psychological rather than physical.

Many of these serious ultra runners have strict diets with no refined sugars and consume only mono and polyunsaturated fats, omega-3's, no trans fat or hydrogenated oils or whatever chemical names that emerged from their diet. There were no chips, no fries, no cookies, nor popcorn. They were all carrying their water in these rubbery "bladders" behind their backs and they took in their hydration through a long tube which I never understood how they could actually wash them.

25 kilometres in the trails is a long way. My race partner, Martin was an experienced road runner. His knee band would have shown you the amount of experience he carried in the field of running. I was typically carrying my bottle of hydration on hand while carrying one bottle in a pouch at my waist. My friends, Cathelin and her husband Gil, with their ruggedness and fun streak in them, had vast interest in trail running. We had a quick chat before we wished one another good luck. Richard who was at the side supporting us kissed me. And off we went.

"Why do you need to carry so much water? It is only 25 kilometres!" exclaimed Martin.

"Let me carry that for you!" He shouted as he grabbed my bottle away.

I was prepared to run and maintain a pace that could probably last the entire distance. I stayed focused, one step at a time. When I faced an upslope, I laid low and pushed myself up before quickly breaking into a quicker jog again during the flats and downslopes. The section near the northern trails was always tougher due to higher humidity and there was no wind. Fortunately, running in such familiar terrain helped a little.

After two hours of running, I just could not comprehend all that about breathtaking natural scenery and lush rainforests. All I saw were just branches, dead leaves, grasses, mud and stones. I felt sticky and smelly with all the perspiration, mud in my socks and granite stones in my shoes.

Soon, Martin was running ahead of me and I found myself running alone about 200 metres behind him. At some exits of the trail, we were blessed with water stations. I took a quick sip, poured the water on my head and continued. At least that made me felt that I was still sane.

Under the heat and high humidity, here I was running
The North Face trails of Singapore.

With directional signages and distance markers, I looked forward to hydrating myself with ice-cold isotonic drink at the next aid station. Many runners were facing the mental challenge. Legs were aching and protesting with every step. As the sun came out in full force, the weather was just getting hotter. After a particular water point, I looked at the bottle Martin was holding. It was reduced to more than half. He had been drinking my water!

All doubts were starting to creep back to the weaker runners. You could ask a thousand whys but you were already in the mid of the forests. There was no turning back. As I chugged along slowly, I started to get worried on the lack of hydration, Richard came from the mid of the forested area and supported us with more hydration.

Although I dreaded running through the toughest parts of the hills, mentally all I could do was to keep going forward. On the rocky terrains, I slowed down to a walk. I saw one man with a single leg amputee in his prosthetic leg standing at one corner and trying to catch his breath. I looked at myself; I had to go on.

At about 8 kilometres from the finishing line, Martin ran out of water and I was just carrying half a bottle of water. Soon, I caught up with Martin as his fatigue set in. Knowing we would not have sufficient hydration til the end of the race, I updated Richard on our location.

The hills were full of other park users. So it was always encouraging to hear shouts of cheers when you were running out of energy and full of exhaustion. Martin was a quiet runner, so I found someone else to talk to along the way. We talked about all the food and desserts we could think of to push ourselves towards the finishing point. Near the end, I could see the light shining through the trails. The finishing line was just ahead. After enduring so many testing hours, I sprinted with my heavy footsteps.

Martin and I completed The North Face 2010.

After about thirty minutes, I saw Cathelin and Gil. They too have finished the North Face. We stumbled onto the ground, glaring and grimacing wildly at the pains we had gone through.

———❖———

Did I like running these trails? I wasn't too sure but Richard had started to wonder if we could complete an ultramarathon. I recognised that running any distance more than 42 kilometres would be called an ultramarathon. Richard knew that the MR25 (MacRitchie 25) Ultramarathon would be happening right after Christmas, and he was tempted to sign us up. Eventually, he did register us for the race. This just sounded ridiculous to go for a race when most people are taking their breaks during the Christmas season! This ultimately became our "A" race for the year.

Training for an ultramarathon took us to another new level. I live in a city where there is traffic every single day. I don't live on vast desert expanses or fields of mossy or rocky boulders, so running half the day on trails was not something I look forward to. Soon, I came to learn that I had to finish five loops, each of about 10 kilometres around the reservoir for this ultramarathon.

On race day, the sun rose early that morning, and it was 30 degree Celsius. Being not a very fast runner, I stayed at the mid of the pack near the starting line. The horn then went off, and we made our way through the bushes. Just like the trails in The North Face race, the initial 8 kilometres of the route was all uphill. I was grateful for the many hours spent in training and running on undulating grounds. It definitely paid off as I climbed through the hills.

With aid stations located about five kilometres apart and filled with huge number of volunteers, they appeared to be angels sent by heaven, and we were thankful with all the hydration and support especially after we had run over kilometres on these treacherous terrains. After completing one loop, I started to have runners passing me, but that did not bother me too much. I was still running a decent pace of less than 8 minutes per kilometre pace. It was not a very fast pace but I had to pace myself as I still had several rounds to go!

As we returned to the starting point to continue another loop, Chris and a couple of running mates were shouting and cheering for me. I talked to myself to keep going. At upslopes, I took short breaks by counting and walking a certain number of steps. After about five hours, I still had one last loop to go. I was extremely happy and in fact pumped up.

I was glad my digestion worked well. Earlier this year, I noticed I was getting a little lactose intolerant. Perhaps it could be my age or my anxiety over a race that I found myself rushing to the toilet after a cup of latte on a race morning. My tummy was also sensitive to certain brands of electrolytes and gels. But all was good now. I was still an hour ahead of the cut off. On the final turn towards the forest exit, it started to pour. Some of the faster runners were still walking.

"Let's finish this!" With the blisters on my feet, the soaked socks, and muddy shoes, I ran along with them.

I was over the moon, I cried at the finish, and I was totally drenched. It had been a long day of close to seven hours. I had not eaten a decent meal, I had not peed, and I had not showered. I could not understand why I was doing this. But I did it anyway. All I knew was that I was officially an ultramarathoner.

Part 2

Becoming the Iron Spirit

Chapter 8

Learning to Swim

After all these running sessions and lucky wins at some of these races, I chanced upon the concept of cross-training from all my reading. Cross-training happens when a runner trains by doing another kind of fitness workout. As part of active recovery and giving my weary legs a break from all that pavement pounding, cross-training like swimming acts as an anti-inflammatory therapy for my legs under cool waters. It helps strengthen some of my non-running muscles and rest my running ones. More importantly, it helps to reduce the chance of injury especially when I was clocking up to about 80 to 90 kilometres per week.

When I first wanted to start swimming as part of cross-training, I had some fears to conquer. Swimming scared the hell out of me. As a child, I had a nagging fear of entering an empty changing room alone. As I grew up, I was even more afraid of falling in, injuring myself falling in, being intoxicated by the highly-chlorinated waters or simply just getting myself into trouble in the waters. Now, as a grown-up adult at 1.55-metre tall, I was not afraid to swim but I was afraid of not touching the bottom of the pool! This just sounded silly to anyone, doesn't it? What happened to all the articles I read about relaxing my body while receiving all the physical and emotional benefits swimming could bring me? There is no secret formula: I had to say yes to let in these possibilities.

I was working five days a week, up to twelve hours a day. Chris who was in the other side of the office would often come over to visit me at work. As usual, we talked about the old days and our runs. During this time, I spoke to Chris about picking up swimming again.

"The pool is just opposite the office. You could have done so easily", he continued.

It was a hot afternoon lunch time and there was absolutely no noise. It was just me, and perhaps a few men in an entire Olympic-size swimming pool. As I entered the side of the pool on the first lane, I had not grown much taller. When I reached the bottom of the pool, I stood still. There was barely enough clearance for me to breathe through my nose, while holding onto the side of the pool with my other hand. I also tiptoed to see if I could see the other end of the pool.

As I pushed myself off from the wall, I was not looking at the black tiles that ran down the lanes. My eyes were in fact focused on the edge of the pool every few seconds to ensure I could hold onto it when I needed to. So here I was swimming a few metres, stopping for a few seconds, taking a few breaths of fresh air, and yet holding to the side of the pool.

As I attempted to finish swimming an entire length, I encountered a swimming training session in the midst of it. I tried not to interfere into their swimming paths. I swam mid-way and stopped by the sides.

"Why did you stop?" Their coach asked me.

"I don't think I can reach the other side of the pool." I was panting away while responding to him.

"You just lack confidence. Try to go slow and see if you can reach the other side." He smiled.

"Alright, I shall try."

Surprisingly, I tried to swim and told myself not to stop until I reach the other side of the pool. I was almost through to the other side which was less than three metres away, before I heard cheers of students. These were the sounds made by the coach's students. I succeeded and I continued for another lap.

And so, this was it. I believed I had recalled the swimming technique I learnt in the past, or at least it was good enough to keep myself afloat with all the arms, splashes and all the tons of energy I had expended. I was definitely panting hard but I swam.

Every lunch time soon became a door of opportunity for me. With a new sense of target setting and purpose, I would quickly run across my office to the pool, put on my swim gears, and swim a few laps. In fact, I felt so pumped up in spending up to two to three times a week in the pool just to shave off seconds or at times, a millisecond. Two laps became four, and soon four became ten. The cross-training I was talking about seemed to have grown to become training of some sorts for the swim leg of a triathlon.

A triathlon consists of a swim, cycle and run. I did not know how long the distance of a swim leg would be, but I knew that to complete a triathlon, I got to finish step one - the swim. I gave myself a lot of pep talk, and not letting fear stop me. Every swimming session consumed my thoughts every second of my lunch time to just achieve that unimaginable goal time.

If I have the will to work hard, I will get better every single day, and every day will be a better day.

This principle stood by me every single day. Now it has also pushed me through the grueling practices in life.

After weeks of swimming, I was not really bothered with the overly chlorinated water and smell of chlorine all over my body. The tan lines on my body spoke for themselves.

———◆———

Please excuse my naivety. After knowing I could swim laps in the pool, I felt I could probably have a go for an aquathlon. I know nothing would happen if I did not take any further action. Here was what I thought I needed to push myself further: registering for the local Tribob Aquathlon which consisted of a 750-metre swim and a 5-kilometre run.

There was only one problem: swimming 750 metres now was not in the pool. It was out in the open sea, and yet I hardly even see the sea since young. When young, my parents rarely brought us to the beaches for they feared that I would be swept away by the waves. I guessed this was timely for my growth.

How different would it be swimming in the pool and out in the sea?

Not knowing the unknown, I was not so afraid of being drowned but I was more fearful of not swimming straight. The aquathlon was happening in a few weeks' time. Rather than getting extremely nervous and worried before the swim, I confronted the swim head on. I just had to look for someone to accompany me to swim out there in the sea. Finally, after much pleading, I sought the help from a friend of Chris who happened to be a lifeguard. His name is Zam.

Without delay, Zam brought me to the beach. The water temperature was about 30 degree Celsius. Despite our hot and humid temperature, I still felt cold as I placed my fingers into the waters. Zam took a rope tied one end to a styrofoam board, and then tied the other end onto one of my legs. As I inched into the cold waters, I noticed my chest felt tighter than usual. Before I swam, I placed my hands in the waters, touched my face, and then pat some more water onto my chest to curb my nerves.

"You swim from this end to the other end and back. Let's see." Zam gestured.

With my bare feet, I slowly walked into the waters until I could not feel the shore. I then started to swim. The feeling of swimming in the open waters was indescribable. Somehow deep within me, I felt I had something to prove.

Mum, you said I should not go to the beach to swim because we do not know how to swim. Now I could swim in the open waters!

My mind was playing this over and over again. This was simply mind-blogging, accompanied with the floating feeling I just had above the waters! I was so happy, kept splashing the waters everywhere, and hugged Zam. This marked another significant change in my life.

I was feeling cold with my first touch of open waters.

———◆———

Races like aquathlons and triathlons come in different distances. Unlike the hundreds of races held in Australia, Europe or The United States, Singapore as a small city with heavy traffic does not hold such races frequently.

I felt blessed to be able to participate in Tribob Aquathlon. The day of the aquathlon finally arrived.

I had my race number stamped onto my arms and legs with some black ink. I always admire triathletes having their body marking done. It means that this man could swim, cycle and run. It did not matter whether I could cycle. Today, it was my turn to have my body marking done. I was blowing at the ink ensuring the numbers would not run.

With a checklist, I put on my timing chip on my left ankle. I strapped it tightly with my Velcro, as I knew the time would be recorded electronically when I crossed the strategically placed timing mats in the race. I then placed my shoes and other gear into a plastic box and placed the box within the drawn-up space in the transition area. I had everything arranged in an orderly manner to facilitate a fast transition later on.

I was fascinated with hundreds of other athletes' gears like colourful water bottles, running shoes, race numbers, and towels. In a triathlon's transition area, it is pure bike porn. The different coloured swim caps represented the different waves the athletes be flagged off.

With some sunblock smothered on, a pair of goggles, swimming legsuits which I believed that I would not look too skimpy on, I was ready for my first aquathlon.

As the starting time approached, the anxiety grew. I stood at the back of the group. Being short had its advantages. I was short enough not to know what was happening at the front. I walked to the side of the crowd to see where the first buoy was. Now I just told myself I just needed to go through the motion. Then the horn went off. Chaos.

I could see swimmers hitting one another. I waited a little before I swam out. I too was kicked by the stronger swimmers. As I swam, I remembered my objective was to complete the swim. So, it was a mixture of breaststroke and freestyle in my swim. Among other people's limbs to avoid, seaweed and sea lice touching my body, and even some sun rays into my eyes as I breathed onto one side of my swim, I was actually enjoying my swim in the open waters! I loved the feeling as if I was surfing with my body on the waters.

Amidst the havoc caused by the crowd of swimmers, buoy by buoy, I kicked harder before I touched land and finished my swim in one piece. I was one of the last few coming back, but I was definitely not the last.

Upon reaching the shore, I made for my run out. Once I was on land, running was a breeze for me. I ran towards the transition area, and identified my blue towel. With less than a-minute transition, I put on my shoes and off I went. For a slow athlete like me, a minute saved on the transition could result in me requiring that last minute near the finish line. Now I just needed to finish this run. I lowered my heart rate a little before I sped up subsequently. I was never a strong swimmer, so I was glad I overtook many athletes in the run leg. Shortly after, I sprinted to finish my five-kilometre run.

Finishing an aquathlon was a big step. This meant I could do and complete an open water swim. This experience gave me an opportunity to go a longer distance the next time. Soon, I was swimming longer from 750 metres to 1,000 metres, to 3,000 and then to 5,000. I also started to go to the beaches more often. Swimming had become one part of a triathlon that I had to get through. I started to love the sport with so much to learn and yet allow me to hone my skills.

I participated in mass swims and clocked up my mileage.

Chapter 9

On the Roads

A lot of new terminology entered my vernacular when I started triathlon. What I love about being in this sport is that I always meet inspiring people, enthusiastic athletes, passionate professionals who give me the much needed motivation to get through our obstacles in our lives. Each one had his own life lessons to share.

I remembered sitting down having a cup of coffee with Chris in a café one morning, reminiscing the Aviva Ironman 70.3 Singapore 2010, and watching the professionals running past us. Upon reaching home, I searched the word "Ironman" on the internet.

A full iron-distance triathlon consisted of a 3.8-kilometre swim, a 180-kilometre bike, and a 42-kilometre run. While a 3.8-kilometre swim meant 76 laps in an Olympic-size pool, a 180-kilometre bike meant sitting on my bike saddle pedaling for about 8 hours. That even sounds long while I am describing the distance to anyone.

The world championship of the iron-distance triathlon is the Ironman in Kona, Hawaii. I watched the Kona Ironman, the Ford Ironman (previously called) and every Ironman race I could find. I was fascinated by those athletes who competed in the toughest single-day endurance race. I kept my faith that if I kept on training, I could complete a triathlon one day too.

A few stories sparked me:

Brian Boyle shared his story of his ordeal of a severe car accident and his miraculous comeback.

Sarah Reinertsen, a paratriathlete and the first female leg amputee to complete the Ironman World Championship in Kona proved to people she could do what other people thought that she could not do.

Scott Rigsby and Rudy Garcia-Tolson were all unique amputated athletes who shared their failures and successes. They started with a decision and the desire to never quit, no matter what happened.

Team Hoyt, where the father Rick Hoyt brought his son Dick who suffered from cerebral palsy to the finish line, demonstrated the power of love of a father.

There are so many stories that make one think whether handicapped or non-handicapped ones are more inspirational. Then, there are those professionals and non-professional athletes. Different people are inspired in different ways. So, should I be bothered with how these people had led their lives? Many of such questions often float in my mind.

Perhaps I should be contented. However, with contentment, I asked myself whether I was happy or disappointed with what I had achieved so far in my life. The challenge now was to look for opportunities to learn and grow, and the motivation to keep moving ahead in life. I had redefined my perceived limits in sports and identified how it could help me in my life.

This marked the beginning of my triathlon passion. Now, I could run and swim, I could now proceed to work on my bike leg in a triathlon.

After a running session one day, I asked Chris to teach me to cycle.

"Why the sudden interest in cycling?" He asked.

"Um..Um…I have signed up for a duathlon which consisted of a run, a bike, then a run", I sheepishly replied.

He laughed off. Without delay, we quickly arranged for a day, rented a bicycle and he brought me to a quiet corner of a park near the beach.

"Hop on, go on, and ride!" Chris exclaimed.

"You have to stand next to me, and run fast enough to catch me!" I insisted. "I know you are a speedy runner!"

Slowly and determined, I crossed over the bicycle with my right leg, tip-toed on the ground, while my genitals hit the top tube of my bicycle. *Ouch!*

I placed my right leg on the right pedal, and hurriedly brought my left leg to step onto the left pedal, making a huge attempt to cycle. In less than five seconds, I fell. I could see the shock in Chris's face. It was official: I could not cycle at all.

Over the next few days, Chris trained along with me on my rented bicycle. With Chris being a fast runner, I was fortunate that I had him catching me whenever I was about to fall. It was not long before I started to grow comfortable on the bicycle.

This was my first ride on a rented bicycle.

After several days of riding, I felt it made a lot more sense buying a road bike which could probably last me several races than paying daily rental charges for the bike I had been training on. I had dreams of cycling a cool-looking bike, just like that of the famous Kona Champion, Chrissie Wellington.

I started by asking around a few friends who were more familiar than me on bikes, and asked for recommendations. Chris accompanied me in my frantic search for the perfect bike. With a tight budget on hand, I even went online, and looked at secondhand bikes, all of which were just too big for me. Nevertheless, we continued our search.

We came across one of the bike rental stores. The store manager approached Chris and asked, "How may I help you?"

"Oh, not me. I have this friend here who is looking for a bike of her size. Do you have any?" Chris promptly replied.

"Hmmm. What kind of bike are you looking at?" The manager looked at me, up and down as if there was something wrong with me. He then walked towards a mountain bike, and was about to recommend me one of those bikes.

I quickly replied, "A road bike or a triathlon bike."

The manager looked perplexed, laughed, and then explained that it was going to be a challenging task to get one for my size. He did not believe that I was a sincere buyer. The following few shops we went to also did not give us any positive response. Some made excuses that they ran out of stock. Some did not even bother to look at me. I did not like that at all.

On one of our last attempts, we drove to a familiar shop. The retailer recommended an Orbea road bike with 650c wheels which could probably fit me. A typical road bike consists of 700c wheels. Following that day, we returned and the retailer made a few adjustments. I found that this bike could probably make it and I made the purchase for it. I had no other choice. The race was just a hundred days away. So upon purchase we made training plans and the training on the road bike started right away the next morning.

I woke up early at four in the morning. Chris picked me up, and went to the same park where we usually trained. I remembered my first training session on my road bike. It was tough: It was a completely different feeling from cycling a mountain bike with balance, gearings, pedaling, and traffic to worry about.

"I don't have much time left, Chris. The duathlon is happening in less than a hundred days!" I was definitely feeling frustrated.

Chris could feel my anxiety as I screamed away but he remained quiet.

All of a sudden, I loaded myself with a crash course on a series of new terminology in cycling: The left shifters adjust the front gears; right shifters adjust the back gears. I remembered what the retailer had been repeating to me. No one told me what the front or back gears do. When Chris asked me to feel my gear, I grew irritated when I could not feel what I was supposed to feel. In fact, I kept looking down at my gears to see where my gears were.

Without further making any noise, Chris led me to cycle a stretch of about 20 kilometres down the park. Making u-turns seemed like a daunting task for me. After repeated failures on the u-turns, I decided to come down and push my bike at the u-turn in the race if I needed to.

After only two sessions, I grumbled to Richard over the discomfort on my bike, and how slow a learner I was. He subsequently did some adjustments on my bike – the tilt of my seat, height of the handlebars, and my reach on the brakes.

"I think I must cut the wire on your handle brakes, and switch the thumb shifters from my bike to yours. You can then easily reach them", explained Richard.

Although thumb shifters were going obsolete, they were Richard's favourite gear-shifting solution for swept back handlebars. With just a twist of his hands with the index finger knuckling against the levers, Richard demonstrated his shifters on his old bike as the cable tension released the motion.

"This would be simple, intuitive and unobtrusive", he proudly explained.

"You know what you are doing?" I asked. He nodded.

Although I admitted I was feeling a sense of discomfort, I placed my trust in him. He then proceeded to do his things on the bike.

Minutes later, things then went wrong. Richard had cut the wrong wire and could not reconnect them back. Left with no choice, Richard brought the bike back to the retailer. By then, Richard could feel my whole load of frustrations. Cycling just wasn't as much fun for me anymore.

After I received my bike from the mechanic two weeks later, Chris and I committed to a minimum of three weekday rides of about an hour and a half each. In our initial rides, stones, debris, dust, leaves and insects were flicking up from the roads. Despite all the marketing hype on the design and polycarbonate materials of popular lens, I chose a pair of safety shades with water-repellant and anti-fog features from an expo. I just could not rationalise paying for almost half the price of my bike for a pair of branded shades.

After several sessions of training, I started to build up some fitness riding on my bike. I also learnt to get into a steady rhythm, meaning I had to consistently pedal on my bike. On the bike, there was much work to be done to master the balance between the gearing and the cadence. It was also a balance between not getting too fast a speed while pedaling and bouncing on my saddle, and not going too slow such that I was grinding in too heavy a gear.

Without doubt, I felt some soreness on my quads, glutes and calves. With the excess fat on my thighs and ass, the fabric on my cloths was rubbing between my saddle and my body, causing lots of discomfort. I got lucky and got a pair of those heavily padded bike shorts at a clearance sale in a retail store. Well, I would not say it was all smooth-going, but at least I was cycling.

One early morning, we cycled up a bridge. I could feel the wind passing me. Soon, I was adding bursts of speed to my workout, working on quick accelerations. As I went up the narrow slope of the bridge, I failed to brake early. I hit against the side of the bridge and fell. I flew about three metres away with my chest hit against the ground. At that moment, I felt as if I could not breathe. I stood up and tried to breathe hard. Trying to calm myself down, I walked around. Chris realised I fell only much later. I was lucky I only suffered a few bike rashes. We then grew to be careful in our next few subsequent rides.

──◈──

On race day, I was feeling excited: It was my first duathlon. I diligently studied my race guide. Each participant was assigned a few stickers consisting of our race numbers – each to be affixed to the bike and bike helmet. While there were some who preferred to wear their race number on their tri top, I wore mine on an elastic race belt around my waist.

The race started with a three-kilometre run, and everyone was already sprinting away. I did a consistent run of about 6.5 minutes per kilometre pace, reached the transition, put on my helmet, and hopped onto my bike in the lightest gear in preparation for the slope ahead. The 15-kilometre bike course consisted of three loops of undulating 5-kilometre off road. It was a single narrow lane, and overtaking any cyclist required certainty.

Just like what I had trained for, I kept to the left while the faster cyclists overtook me on the right. Cycling then became an aggressive sport as the faster cyclists started shouting "To your right!" or "Keep left!" as they flew past me. Any unsteady ride could result in possible collision. These cyclists were serious!

I did not really bother about the location of the aid stations. I was still not confident of taking my hands off my handlebars to take my drink or even scratch an itch. I felt like a camel with my one- litre hydration bag on my back. I had the tube in my mouth at all times to ensure I could drink off from the bag.

As I slowly made my turns at the u-turn, I heaved a sigh of relief at my last loop as I made my way back to the transition. At a state of confusion while trying to catch my breath, I could not find my bike slot. I was very much tempted to just hang my bike anywhere along the pole. After losing a few minutes, I found my bike position. Suddenly, I felt the weight of my machine. I made a quick transition, and ran out. My legs felt like a ton of bricks. I looked at my feet, and they were definitely still there. I just continued going, which by then, I knew I could finish this race. I learnt from Richard after the race that many athletes who were going at too fast a speed actually fell at the sharp u-turns. I felt blessed that I finished Tribob Duathlon safely.

It was amazing what a cup of good coffee could lead to. I was celebrating my completion with Chris and Richard. Our conversations then went from duathlons to triathlons. We toyed with the idea of perhaps someday competing in a triathlon. But we knew nothing would happen if we procrastinate any further.

I was riding with the big boys in a duathlon race.

And so I did proceed to join a few other races involving runs, duathlons and sprint distance triathlons. I too had my falls, felt banged up, and devastated about the bike course, my bike and eventually my own bike handling skills. In triathlon, there would not be a second thought. For me to catch up, I just have to keep improving and keep moving forward.

*I suffered a fall when a rider suddenly braked in
front of me in a mass cycling event.*

We heard the Aviva Ironman 70.3 was about to end its term in 2012 in Singapore. This was also the moment when I gathered my friends to participate as a team. The support was simply encouraging. It was simply surprising what spurred me to start a triathlon actually gave me a time for self-reflection. I was always ahead in terms of my developmental growth and planning of my life.

Signing up for races is not too tough as long as you have the money and the will to start and finish them. The sport has definitely instilled some form of discipline in my life such as uncluttering the race packs, washing the soiled clothes, sorting out the unpaired socks and accessories, and downloading the event photographs and data from my equipment.

I separate my triathlon world from my working world. I literally have my time for each activity boxed up and remained focused at work. It was getting increasingly difficult especially when it was getting more obvious that I had better knowledge of the sports domain than most of my colleagues and clients during conversations at work.

I had colleagues discussing their vacation plans while others tried to catch up on their sleeping or with their Korean drama series. Other than going for races, I also took leave to attend to World Athletes appointments, media photoshoots, courses and sports networking sessions to enrich myself further.

Through sports, I found a balance in life.

———◆◇◆———

Chapter 10

Pains and Aches

Constantly thinking about running, swimming, cycling, duathlons and triathlons could be nerve-wrecking. It seemed that they were not the only things in life, yet at times, they took up so much of the time in my life. So, I often appreciate the other side of my life – people who are dear and important to me in my life. Without doubt, I have close friends in this sport. Whether I was discussing about dynamics or relationships between people or exploring about opportunities out there, I had various friends who would give me insights especially when my mind was all so soaked up with all the training. I never stopped having conversations with my friends too – learning their life stories, some of which I could relate to.

Richard is a simple guy. Just like many couples who will say their partners complete them, Richard simplifies me. I was neither a cyclist nor a triathlete when he first knew me. He has supported and built me up just like how he has built his bike. In early 2011, when we were going to get married, I was rushed by my parents to pack everything in my house, and leave nothing in the house. These were what my parents wanted.

Eventually, I got married, stayed with Richard in his new apartment, and left my parents' place. This became another phase of my life. After I left my parents' place, I realised that my parents who had been staying together with me for so many years had changed. My dad became more individualistic and was spending more time in the temple than that at home. Despite receiving my messages, my dad somehow had not kept in touch with me. He had kept to himself all these years. As for my mum, she had been staying at home doing household chores all these years. When my dad and her children are not around at home, my mum has our support, and learns to be self-independent.

On my weekly dates with my mum, she shares with me stories about how my dad had used harsh words on her, how my dad had supported my sister even when she was in the wrong, and every other things she could pick on. There seemed to be so much baggage. As much as I would like my mum to stay away from all these unhappiness, I just could not afford to get another apartment for my mum to live in. Neither could I consistently send her on travelling trips. Time is just something I take out of myself and listen to her while nurturing my inner self.

Unknowingly, Richard had picked up almost all the burden I was carrying – the history of my family, my extended family, and the dreams that I once held so tightly as a child. He never asked for any of these, not even before our wedding day.

After six months into our marriage, he finally asked, "How do you feel when your dad treats you like that?"

"Why is your family behaving as if they cannot wait to get you out of the house? Why are they so urgent and so eager to get you to pack all your clothings and items?"

I smiled at him.

"Does it bother you?" I asked him.

I replied telling him that if it did not bother me, it should not bother him too.

"I cannot control how others think of me. What can I say or do will actually stop them? And do you really think it will stop them?" I continued.

As I became a mature adult, I know my loved ones will say anything they please. I don't hate them.

I know how my life has been and how challenging the world has become. Life is tough and that is a given. There are no magical fixes. I have only two choices. I can choose to sulk about them, or I keep moving forward. I never give in, and I learn to grow beyond them as there is still so much in life I have to work on. I love them but I have to live my own life. I believe we are all powerful beyond measure.

For the first few years after marriage, one of the most common questions we faced as a couple was whether we had any children. I grew into my thirties, and I slowly realised that I might be reaching an age group which I might not conceive easily. During our first visit to our gynaecologist, Richard and I were definitely overwhelmed over the anxiety of the couples. Some looked happy. Some looked too painful to share. The doctor gave me a healthy bill. I guessed I just needed plenty of luck. I was sure my worst days were someone else's best. I felt lucky enough that I had no terminal illnesses or any financial bankruptcy. Neither did I want to place too much unnecessary stress on Richard. Even if I had a child now, I was very clear that I did not want a child to grow up having a childhood like that of mine.

What was my childhood like?

I spent a lot of time with my grandpa before I was three. I miss my grandpa. I lost him when I was three. It was because of my dad's busy schedule, and the strained relationship between my mum, my grandma, and all the other family matters that I got to bond closer with my grandpa. As I grew older, I grew closer to my mum's mum.

Yet now, from my mum's side, my grandma's health had also deteriorated. I hardly met my grandma who could not walk much. I was also on the verge of burn out from all my work and training.

"Your brother and I are going to Taiwan next week", my mum was sharing with me excitedly. I hardly borrow my brother's car as it was his beloved possession.

"You can have the car", my brother told me.

The week after came. Richard and I somehow just decided to make a two-hour trip down to the hospital in my brother's car. I was not sure of the location of the hospital but my gut feel told me it was opportunistic to meet her, and we eventually managed to find it.

"Ah Ma!" That was a familiar address my grandma had longed for as I shouted across the hospital beds.

My grandma's hardship through the World War II, her resilience working as a servant for the various British families, her lack of wealth, and how she had lived in the different homes of my uncles – these were stories I heard from my grandma. My grandma used to cook the best dishes ranging from American pork chops to Peranakan curries to Chinese fried rice.

For that moment, it was a painful sight for me. It appeared that my grandma had been transformed overnight from someone who used to be so strong in character to someone who had been overpowered by illnesses. I held her warm hands, yet I could see the bruises from all the injections and distended veins. People had often said about a person with the greatest possessions would end up with nothing when one suffered an illness. This seemed so true now for me. Richard then took a picture of my grandma and me. That was the last time I saw her. She passed away soon after.

The way I see it, the difficulties that the triathlon world had put me through would never be anything like as significant as these tragic times. My grandma's death was a moment of personal reflection coupled with determination

I found peace within myself: I told myself that it was time to let go. I had to be fair to Richard and tossed my past out of the window. I moved on with one idea in mind: try to do all I can to be happy in life.

Life is short, and that is a reality.

⁕⬥⁕

While I had let nature take its course, there were times when I was tied between the choice of completing a full iron-distance triathlon or focusing on setting up a family. Yet there were also many other considerations that did not clearly show me the light.

After the fall from the bridge and completion of my duathlon, I had also stopped cycling. First, I blamed it on the bike. Then I also blamed about not having a safe place near my home to train my cycling. I also had a nagging fear that my parents would not be happy with me if I were to bring my bike back home. I had tons of excuses not to cycle. After a few months of hiatus, I knew it was just me. I thought I was done with cycling, and had experienced enough of these races.

Yet inside me, I was still making a trip down several kilometres to support races. I did not want to miss any event that was happening. It was if I had very much wanted to be part of the triathlon family. I just did not know how to start it again.

To kick-start the adrenaline in us, Richard and I signed up for several ten-kilometre races and half marathons. We grew ambitious, and joked at the possibility of winning something. We even signed up for a vertical marathon, trained hard, and aimed to do our best. We were definitely not fast athletes, so was it all possible?

The course of a vertical marathon never fails to amaze me. The layout of the stairwell was just amazing – going clockwise and anti-clockwise on half of the floors, before mapping to clockwise route on various parts of the course with a variety of four to seven flight arrangements, straining every muscle on both our legs and arms in pulling ourselves up. Part of the thrill included lowly-ventilated floors, with fire doors opened every few floors to allow blowers to blow for better ventilation. We heard cheers as we climbed up every floor. Then it all became noise as the challenge increases, and it was just our minds which kept ourselves going. Considering we were fighting with the teenage students and the veteran runners, we applauded ourselves for winning the seventh position.

Now, it seems that anything is possible. Our talents are directly connected to our passions. It is possible to be gifted in something you are passionate about. And when we have the courage to follow our passions, we will excel in what we do because we invest our whole energy into it. We will just make it happen.

When all things started to light up in my journey towards triathlon, my story took another shocking turn.

One night after I came home from work, my eyes went sore. I had been rubbing them the whole day at work. I had taken off my contact lenses, but my eyes were still itching. That night, I could hardly open my eyes. I thought I could just sleep them off as I was feeling too tired after all the rubbing. The next day, my eyes were hurting so badly that I had to see my doctor. He made his regular checks and appeared anxious.

"You have constricted blood vessels in your eyeballs. You can go blind!" he exclaimed.

"Oh come on, they can't be so serious. You must be joking." I responded calmly to the doctor.

The doctor then took a few pictures of my eye with his instrument, and showed me how close the constricted blood vessels were from the black part of my eyes. It then became so technical with all his explanations. Then, everything just happened so fast. My doctor immediately made an appointment at the eye hospital and urged me to rush down without delay. I did not even have the time to tell Richard, my boss or anyone else!

After the visit to the eye hospital with several checks, I was given a strict schedule of follow-ups, care, and cleaning procedure for my eyes. During these darkest times (literally), with all the medication in my eyes, everything was in a blur. In the office, I could not see anything on the screen during presentations. But I acted as per normal at work. I did not want to attract any unwanted attention. I still did my usual stuff like running, though I could not really tell what was ahead of me. The only lines I could see on the roads were the yellow brighter ones which guided me in my runs.

It took me about five months for the complete healing of my eyes. I was not allowed to wear contact lenses anymore. I had to start everything from scratch. My old prescribed spectacles did not work for me, and it actually took several prescriptions before my optician could get my pair right. My eyes took a while to adapt to the light. Instead of going through the laser treatment for my eyes, I chose the cheaper alternative of using a new pair of spectacles, and put aside all my beloved shades which I had been wearing. As my eyes prescription was just too high, I could not go for the prescribed shades. The only alternative was the use of clip-on lens. I also started to use optical goggles for my swim.

My eyes did not stop me from what I wanted to do. Of course, I was restricted by external demands that life imposed on me. I was a married working executive with bills to pay and family commitments to shoulder. I too have to do what was necessary to survive. Life is not just about survival. It is about joy, fulfilment, growth and in search of meaning, inner peace, and giving back to the world. I believed I have this real talent worth which is to keep on being inquisitive and being mindful, wondering about the world and then taking every possible opportunity to create excitement and meaning to my life. To enjoy every minute, whether it is writing a book, giving a speech, drinking a cup of coffee, feeding my fish, it will be my life. If these are what we want, more will come.

My return to the sport of triathlon reminded me that my decision to keep racing was not mine alone. No words could describe Richard's anxiety whenever he signed up a race for me or how he set up the various bike parts for me in preparation for a race.

When we got married, we lived about a few kilometres near the beach. I had no excuse not to ride. We started everything from scratch – buying a mountain bike, taking off, learning to pedal, gaining momentum at an optimal body position, braking slowly, and stopping along tight roads and slopes. This time round, I had clear outcomes for every training session. Of course, there were times I still felt I had too many stuff to watch out for but I was improving. I was gaining my confidence on my bike back.

With the newly-equipped cycling skills, I felt like a child with a whole load of adventures in my mind. Richard and I started to look for interesting UNESCO World Heritage sites. Our first adventures took us to Phnom Penh Cambodia. One of the interesting sites was Oudong Mountain, which was in the tentative list of UNESCO sites.

To get to Oudong Mountain, we could enjoy a bike ride there or take a taxi trip. Partly as an excuse to feast on the various curries and cuisines of Cambodia, I had also wanted to do some distance cycling for a very long time. We made a quick research of organised bike tours and found a 55- kilometre long bike ride. With the newly-found interest in riding, I thought I was lucky they carried the smallest bike for me, with the saddle all the way down and all the way to the front.

55 kilometres is just slightly longer than a marathon.

This was how I was playing my mind, and this could perhaps be my first longest bike ride.

Cycling from the town to OuMountain was a bad choice. Coming from a very structured country like Singapore, I was overwhelmed with the chaotic roads of Phnom Penh. While a huge number of vehicles drove on the left lane, the motorcyclists and cyclists were still going everywhere. While the clanky, rusty old town bikes could go any direction, there were many who nonchalantly carried vast loads on the bikes. Loads of live chicken, layers of bananas and leaves, and a family of five --- these were all stacked behind the cyclist. We cycled past the back roads and hills. While the roads were in relatively good shape, the dustiness of the Cambodian countryside just proved too overwhelming.

Very good it had been: friendly people, lovely scenery, frequent roadside stalls selling fruits and raw foods. We cycled past the old railway station, with a few pedal strokes into the open rice fields and villages. While cycling on the small trails and backroads, I could not help but to smile back to the friendly kids who were waving to us as we rode. It was common as we freewheeled downhill, round corners and overtaking a truck. And we saw an ox in the midst of the roads with a pile of poo right in front of me!

On such busy roads, signs were rare. Road markings were non-existent at traffic junctions, and along streams. They were not the kind of roads where we would look to our left, right and back to our left again. Vehicles were merging everywhere. We just simply moved forward, got into the traffic, and kept moving till we were on the other side of the road. While we might see motorcyclists wearing helmets, it was not common to see cyclists riding with helmets.

After cycling for about 30 kilometres across huge puddles of water and trails, I was tired. I had just eaten a bowl of noodles that was the size of a huge soccer ball. I continued on this sandy stretch feeling exhausted and irritable, hoping I could get some balance riding through the sands. Feeling detached from the front of the group consisting of one Australian strong-looking matured guy and another well-toned tall and skinny guy, Richard was also in front of me. I made a slow solitary push to the end of the stretch, squinting my eyes through the dust, and endured. Then the Australian guy came over and advised me to go at a low gear and spin faster to get myself out of the sandy pitch. On our way towards the 40-kilometre mark, my bike seemed to quiet the terrain. It made the hard moves that made me feel more powerful, offering a stability that kept me focused on the ride. It did well, as we approached this historic temple site, I could still keep it in a big gear. I was very much assured by the guide when he shared that the bike had made it enjoyable for us to ride on those exhilarating rocks and gravels.

After we reached the base of the hill, we took about few hundred steps up Phnom Oudong. With majestic views of the Cambodian countryside, I took a deep breath while appreciating the flatness of the lands. With the important remnants such as burial sites of Khmer Kings and religious artifacts dating back to hundreds of years, Oudong was such a site.

Travel had indeed opened up my mind, and it had given me insights into other cultures. That stupid self-pity I felt before the ride was gone.

The trails I cycled in Phnom Penh were just an inkling of what I was capable of.

I stopped at a sight in Phnom Penh.

Strange things happened after a month from our Phnom Penh trip: I was pregnant. Somehow within me, I was not feeling happy. Not because I was not happy being a mother, but somehow I felt I could only be relieved after I had delivered the child.

I was not exactly worrying but all of that sudden I was not sure if Richard or I were ready for a child. People often asked, "What's your objective in life?" One could probably say "To earn millions of dollars" or "Feed my family well". No, it is not about getting married, getting a good job or build a good life. To me, these are not what I see as "focus" in life. These are tasks, which anyone rightfully will be doing to beat the rising inflation rates.

While Richard paid the apartment fees, household bills, utility bills, some trips and meals, I saw my partner at the age of mid-forties, gritting his teeth, holding his job tightly til he was given the golden handshake. With current rising apartment prices hitting above S$500,000 for a 40-square metre size and family sedan cars costing above S$100,000, we just could not see how we could find value in owning any of these anymore!

I thought my mum said my future would be brighter when I had my degree. I did not study my way to university and masters to struggle to get a job that could hardly pay my bills, bring up a family of my own, and my growing interest in sports. Everyone is in this rat race. Nearing age forty, I wanted to maximise my potential, be in good health, travel and contribute to a social good. There were all these balance about passion, development and what was happening in reality.

Things did not go as well as they should. Six weeks into my pregnancy, I started to bleed, followed by a series of sharp pain. It happened during a weekend, and my clinic was closed. Richard was working that afternoon, and I was all alone. Without hesitation, I gave a call to Richard, and then I dragged myself into the taxi to the hospital. In the taxi, I tried to tolerate the pain and not frighten the driver. At the hospital, I lost more blood in the toilet.

I was not hopeful. I am not a Christian yet I prayed for God to save the child. The doctor injected something in me, and asked me to return days later for some scans and tests. As expected, it became clear that our gorgeous nugget of a baby had left us just like that. The doctor shared that it could be the result of an abnormal chromosome and many other reasons. I am sharing this openly so that others can actually feel they could too.

At that moment, I felt as if I have lost everything – my dad was not communicating with me, my mum and my brother could not understand me, and now even the heaven seemed to be playing with me! I cried for a couple of days, and hid behind my blankets. As Richard tried all ways to make me eat and move on with life, I resisted crying in front of him. It took me as much strength as he did to pull myself up and said I had to fix this and look for the opportunities within this loss.

I was advised by the doctor not to run, not to work and to rest. I went to work as per normal, putting up a strong front when I was actually in pain physically and mentally. While there seemed to be so many things that were going wrong, I was still so fortunate that I had my closed ones with me and so many things that were still going right. I had to move on. My perseverance has been shaped by the challenging conditions in which I have lived in all my life. What else more could I not take?

I could have told my mum, my friends, everyone in the world out there about my loss. But there were already tons of questions being raised by my mum, my brother, friends and even strangers. It did not matter whether we had answers to these questions.

"When are the two of you starting a family?"

"When are you going to stop doing these sports?"

"Have you thought about us when you are doing these triathlon sports?"

Have you ever felt like you wanted to say the truth about a certain matter thinking that the person you spoke to would understand about what you are really trying to say, would understand your situation and understand why you are doing a course of action?

Somehow all these put-downs had to be stopped. As I failed to resonate with my loved ones about their lack of support towards our personal life and interests, I started to focus my energies on what could probably move us towards our goals.

Everyone has a life of his or her own. I understand my mum with her baggage. I grow up hoping my brother would probably learn to appreciate me better – a sister who has been married, how her life has been, and why she is doing what she is doing. I too as a sister have been giving my fullest support to whatever he has been doing in his life.

❈

Two years later, my brother got married. Richard and I were making our second attempt on having a child. After my operation, the doctor had forbidden me to move around. There was no way I was not turning up for my brother's wedding. We asked our nurse to wrap a bandage around my knee faking an injury, so that I would not be moving so much. I had all the questions from the crowd that day but I took them on my stride.

I had seen how much a person could suppress one's emotions and needs, made so many sacrifices for the family, and yet emotionally wrecking oneself while pretending to be strong and that everything being fine. Everyone deserves better. This was a constant reminder and the need for everyone to dissolve our resentful minds and stories that often so drained us before they dissolve us. Just like my mum. She is a living example for me. I too must love myself.

After my loss and unsuccessful attempts, I started to cycle again. Richard and I have placed our time and effort going through the mastery of the triathlon sport. Richard enjoys looking at the bicycles and meeting various people in the sport. Many people have inspired us in our journey as we grew in the sport.

The story must go on.

Chapter 11

Beginning our Overseas Adventures

There are many theories on people who do triathlons. There are people who are filling a gap in their lives, having no commitments like children or families or heavy-burdened jobs and as such they have loads of time and money to spend on the sport. Perhaps there are also those who just need to feel good in accomplishing such a daunting task.

I am a typical busy executive, working close to about fifty-five hours per week, married, and shared all the household chores with my partner. While there are high wage earners who owned S$10,000 worth of bikes, the most expensive set of wheels, equipment and accessories, Richard and I are the average Jack and Jill and remain conservative in our spending. We still take time out with our loved ones along with all the problems that come with them. As I continued my training, the little devil in my mind often played the same questions over and over again.

Why would I need to train and put in the quality and amount of training so hard, and then back up with a challenging day ahead in the office? Why would I sell my working career short with a lack of sleep and probably drop a few more strands of hair or growing a few more white hair?

You loved all these, don't you?

I am as sane as anyone out there.

What kept me going?

I want to get the best out of myself and yet I am just like any other athletes out there working their day jobs and dealing with the same dilemma.

And so we continued our lessons from where we left off. Everything was back to the drawing board.

I also started signing up for a couple of races held by universities and clubs. I was also getting my mileage from the charity racing events. Recovering from my misfortune, I was not as fresh as I had wished on race day for my aquathlon with the Lions Club, but I was determined to do a great race. I told myself that if I did well in this race, I would proceed to sign up for a half iron-distance triathlon. I got third that day.

It seemed that suddenly there was hope in my life. With incremental adjustments of five minutes earlier each day, I woke up at about six in the morning each day, and did my runs or cycling. On days I had sore muscles, I had alternative plans for my training. On days when it started to rain, I was happy I could go back to my bed and grab a few naps. There were days when the rain did not stop our training plans especially on weekends. I had Richard who was always reminding me about training.

"Wheels down, time to ride", shouted Richard.

For a moment, I felt Richard was crazy riding in the rain. There was no way I would be putting down the rubber on the wet road. Yet he persisted and I relented. In the rain, we cycled with care and got ourselves riding through the wet terrains. On days when we were not that crazy, we set up our bikes on our indoor trainers, placed the two bikes in a very congested living room within our 40-square-metre apartment, right in front of the TV, and did our rides while watching his favourite movie.

During weekends, waking up early in the morning could be worse. We forced ourselves to put on our gears, gloves, prepare a couple of hydration, put on road id with a lit helmet and lights, change our shades, grab our first aid kit and puncture kit, pump up the tyres and brave the best of the Singapore hot weather. Most of the time then, Richard just rode while I kept my heart rate low and getting the base mileage in. Once a month, we dug in on the climbs and pushed our heart rate up. Together with Richard, I planned my entire year of "B" and "C" races while enjoying travelling on our own. That was about as structured as it got.

My indicator for success in life was just like that of the sport of triathlon – I swim forward in the choppy waters, I cycle my bike forward in view of the strong headwinds and steep hills, I run forward even my body tells me no more. I just had to force myself moving forward.

With my petite size, we had much difficulty in getting a bike of the right size for me. One day I noticed a photo of a petite lady cycling on a road bike on facebook and tracked right to the store to locate it. It was the last piece of Colnago CLD with the smallest frame size 40. Colnago CLD bike was rarely seen in Singapore as many cyclists had been following the assumingly-better bikes ridden by top triathletes. But this fitted me. With a reasonable price tag, we bought it and named it "Milou". This was the French name for Snowy like the character in the comics Tin Tin which would accompany me through the adventures around the world.

Since my last fall on my old road bike, it took some time for me after a few falls to recall a couple of things about cycling – gear shifting, no cross-chaining, defensive cycling and pedaling.

Weeks later, when I could manage Milou better, it was time for me to come good on a promise I made far too long ago. This would be my fight, the start of my closure and to honour my little one. I signed up for Metaman 70.3, a half iron-distance triathlon in 2013.

We also started to live the life we have responsibly and fully.

This was taken on the top of a hill in one of our Bintan rides.

Despite my efforts in training and all for the Metaman, I was on the verge of slipping back into a very demoralising state especially when demands at work were perpetually increasing. Everyone in my team was burning out. I took breaks over weekends and travelled to neighbouring countries to train, to race and to learn more about people, their cultures and their stories. After experiencing a few local and overseas triathlons, Richard promised a whole new different racing experience in a unique destination combining a luxurious race setting with a challenging course. It is always nice to receive a surprise. Three days before we left, he shared that he had signed us up for the Bali Triathlon.

Bali Triathlon was an overseas Olympic Distance triathlon which included 1.5-kilometre swim in the warm waters of Jimbaran Bay, 40-kilometre bike on hilly paved roads, and 10-kilometre run up the hills. It was a well-organised race, with pre-race briefings, welcome cocktails, reccees, high-carbo race eve dinner, and post-race party celebrations. They even had Balinese bike blessings which included a prayer procedure on our bikes for a smooth ride ahead.

Despite the currents and larger sea waves than those in Singapore, the swim was manageable. Like that of a typical tropical country, there was no visibility in the sediment-filled waters. The waters was also filled with jelly fishes, so we received a few stings here and there. I just felt comforted that I could actually swim amidst such waves. The bike ride was fun with winding narrow roads accompanied with some hills, animals like dogs and oxen, children running around, and some really slow-moving trucks.

With Milou's standard bike parts, I was aware that component retailers like to sell me lots of new parts which can lead to much confusion, even if I did not need them. In reality, the most fanciful parts often do not suit me for my size. Richard had been doing lots of research on the components and we often discussed about them. With Milou's standard Shimano 50/34 chain rings, Shimano 105 12/25 rear cassette and heavier Shimano RS21 wheels, I was having much difficulty on climbing.

Before this Bali triathlon race, Richard had been looking at a compact crank, rear derailleur, cassette and wheels for an easier climb (hopefully). He eventually changed the rear cassette to a Shimano Ultegra 11/28 along with Fulcrum Racing One wheels. I was not sure if Milou could actually carry me through the 15 percent grade climb up certain slopes of Bali, but I did know I was willing to give it a go.

We had many discussions over bike parts, one of which was the bike pedals – platform or clipless, 2-hole Shimano Pedaling Dynamics (SPD) system or 3-hole pedal ones and several other types. All these caused me headaches as I just wanted the best solution in the quickest manner. After experimenting with the various pedals, I found the hybrid clipless platform bike pedals which were meant for mountain bikes perfect for me. This was a good start for me to practice cycling on clipless pedals. Despite all the dangers that came with locking my feet onto these pedals, clipless pedals indeed increased my pedaling efficiency and transferred the power from the leg to the bike more efficiently.

With Milou, I was climbing some of these hills at speed of single digits! My hamstrings felt as if they were almost ripped apart. I started well hydrated because I imagined it would be quite thirsty work in the heat. I rode with two 750 millilitre bike bottles in my bottle cage and lasted me throughout the race.

I was very much encouraged by loud cheers on the sides of the roads. At the traffic junctions, there were about a hundred motorcyclists that looked like mosquitoes waiting for the lights to turn green. With the several horizontal ridges on the roads which made it quite uncomfortable for cycling, I was probably one of the last few trying to cycle along the roads with special care. So the last 20 kilometres was slow for me especially when I had to deploy defensive cycling strategy into the race. While I had my front wheel almost brushing into a motorcycle in front of me, the Bali Police managed to divert a large portion of the overwhelming number of vehicles which were attempting to use the same course. Together with the Police, the local security teams from the communities also assisted in deterring the vehicular traffic. The run was expectedly hot just like in any tropical humid country. I soon slowed down to a walk up the slopes, and poured myself with water. Eventually, I felt strong, and completed the race.

Did you know?

> *We did not stay in the official race hotel. We stayed in a budget hotel which was about three kilometres away. The traffic in Bali was often heavy filled with motorcyclists. Special care has to be taken in cycling through tight roads to and from race venue.*
>
> *Bali is a famed destination for relaxation and culture by travellers worldwide. Aside from being careful on the hygiene and quality of food and drinks, it is always good to take caution as a tourist with respect to extra charges for transporting your huge bike bag on a trolley and phototaking.*

In my life story, I felt I was either writing my best part of my life or my worst part of my life. As much as I was struggling to kick start my half iron-distance triathlon journey, I had a beginning with an end I would like very much thought out to be. But I was also at a loss for what was actually going through in the middle. I was nowhere near the full iron-distance triathlon finisher I very much would like to be.

In order for me to gain more experience in the sport, Richard signed me up for a couple of triathlon races.

The success of Bali Triathlon weeks before led us to this century ride. Iskandar is a newly developed southern part of Johor Malaysia, about 20 kilometres away from Singapore. The 100-kilometre route included nice undulating terrains and highways accompanied with two water stations.

I looked around the few hundreds of cyclists with their bikes around me at the starting line of Iskandar Malaysia century ride. All were tanned, lean-muscled, and looked like they had been training for this ride for a long time. I started to feel worried for Richard and myself.

Does he really know what he has signed us up for? What if we are the only ones left behind?

Being an amateur in cycling, I cycled along the initial part of the route with care at about 22 kilometres per hour on the initial 30 kilometres of rolling hills while the faster cyclists were going above 35 kilometres per hour. While both Richard and I just could not form any groups with these crazy cyclists who by then were going above 40 kilometres per hour, we cycled on near threshold.

Strangely after about 40 kilometres, I felt stronger as I cycled at an average of about 22 to 24 kilometres per hour. I started to overtake some cyclists who were going at too fast a speed at the earlier part of the ride. Cycling over several slopes of about 15 percent grade did take a lot out from me to reach the top of the hills. By then, my hands were sweating against the gloves, and I had to concentrate on keeping my feet moving, and preventing my hands from slipping.

I also cycled up the slopes of about 15 percent grade on many occasions. I was thankful for one of the marshals who was riding beside me throughout the ride till the finish. Although I was one of the last few cyclists who reached the finish line, I was completely satisfied with myself for completing my first century ride.

There I was pleasantly surprised to see Richard who seemed to have finished the ride earlier than me. He responded by saying that the one of the marshals who rode his bike had actually misled him to the wrong route.

Did you know?

> *We rented a car in Singapore to drive into Iskandar Malaysia. Pretty straightforward. It was a new car. We drove into Iskandar, we parked the car at a parallel parking lot just like everyone else and also parked the car at a prominent place where we could minimise carjacking.*
>
> *We returned to the car after the ride only to discover that one of the side mirrors had been smashed. And it was only our car which suffered this damage. We were fortunate we paid the excess charges before we rented the car. We learnt not to choose a new car driving into Malaysia.*

I had my first century ride with a marshal guiding me.

After the Iskandar ride, I was still scared of the road. I had a deal with Richard. I promised to put in some time on the bike trainers, get the base mileage in, all with a view to build my way up to finish the Metaman. Although the trainers made me feel like some sweaty demoralised hamster rolling the pedals away, it allowed me to concentrate solely on what I wanted to do with no traffic road condition or weather woes. I built my training into specific sessions – interval training, easy rides, and blocks of hill reps. I told myself I had to do these if I wanted to make it to the time cut-off.

The strongest motivator for me in completing my rides was thinking of the reward I get: an iced cold glass of coke, or a nice cup of latte or a bowl of truffle fries. A two-hour bike ride in exchange for a piece of that cake in the café once in a while was encouraging. The chicken salad or roasted chicken definitely helped me to recover faster.

———◆———

Chapter 12

What It Takes

It was perhaps a natural progression for me to move to a longer distance triathlon. When I thought I was getting serious in this, I acknowledged swimming as my weakest sport. Swimming was one area I needed to spend a little more time on.

Physically, I was at a disadvantage with my petite frame before we even talked about speed, power and strength. Yet mentally, I was strong enough to know that I could build up my endurance in my swim after finishing several mass and charity swims. Accompanied with the long swims to build up my endurance, I found myself stricken with a runny nose after the swim. Neither did I find it enjoyable to spend hours staring at the bottom of the pool till my fingers went wrinkly.

Attending talks and activities held by clubs, reading up articles in magazines and books, and watching videos on form and techniques, I found execution in the pool as a different matter. Swimming is such a technical sport that I need to turn my body or bring my arms up in a certain way to get myself moving through the waters. With the newfound knowledge, I got myself so excited that I spoke to Richard one night about this.

"I thought swimming is only freestyle, breaststroke, backstroke and butterfly?" I asked Richard. "Who was the one who came up with this front crawl?"

We did a search on the internet. Indeed, it was some Australian who developed the crawl stroke which involved a six-beat kick. Although the front crawl involved one of two long axis strokes, it was not a swimming style officially regulated by FINA (International Swimming Federation). FINA is internationally recognised for administering international competition in Aquatics such as swimming, diving, open water swimming. This front crawl swimming position allowed arm flexibility in the water and arm recovery which reduced drag accompanied with body rolling movement. With all the reading on the ergonomics and history, I looked at Richard.

"Let's admit it", I paused a little.

"Perhaps with your height, you could have the making of a swimmer."

He smiled at me.

"I think I need to learn swimming properly rather than to pretend knowing how to swim like an iron-distance swimmer, spending long hours in the pool."

I had already spent quite a substantial portion of my salary on my monthly gym fees, a new bike, bike parts like clipless pedals, cassette and wheels, new triathlon gears, and races. I did not want to spend a further few hundreds of dollars in getting an expensive swimming coach. So somehow, I chanced upon a website, and settled for an affordable swimming coach.

Weighing over 100 kilograms, this guy named Wardi came to the pool. He looked huge! I just could not imagine his weight being thrown into the waters. I placed my faith in him as he jumped in and swam a few easy metres.

"Would this pool do?" I asked him.

The pool was a 35 metres by 1.5 metres deep pool.

"Why not?" he replied and we began our session.

Just as expected, I had so many errors in my swimming strokes and techniques. Freestyle is about pulling and gliding and I was not doing either. It was a step-by-step progression as I started to see Wardi bringing swimming aids like paddles, buoys, and flippers to the classes. One of the more challenging sessions like the following example actually revealed my weakness.

I had to first complete a 10-minute run on the treadmill. I then rolled onto my back, bent my knees, clasped my hands behind my head and started my sit-ups. I could not do a single decent sit-up!

My abdominals, buried under my fats, burned. I grit my teeth, pulled myself up, and shouted to myself that I could do this no more.

60 second core planks…

60 second side planks. Left. Right.

20 sit-ups…

I remembered every bit of this commando form of training. I continued to swim for about 10m before I came up again. I watched my fingers quaking from fear as I continued to do my push-ups. I bowed my head and faced down.

A minute passed, and another set of lunges came in.

My feet and arms burnt, my hands clenched onto the edge of the side chair as I made my lunges, fighting and trying to maintain the grip while my hands shook.

Blood rose to my head, and my pulse throbbed. I was breathing hard, as if I could not feel my heart beat any more. It was amazing for me to think about how I first resisted swimming when I was seven. Flashbacks of my childhood swimming lessons returned to my mind. Thirty years forward, here I was standing in my own pool, and learning how to swim again

Wardi taught me to recognise the difference between training and racing. It was not easy to learn and execute the right stroke during swim training; let alone on race day. Other than the various kinds of water start he got me ready for, he reminded me that the races demanded much more from me.

"You have to overcome your nerves, be wary of who or what is around you while you continue to focus on your swimming techniques," Wardi explained.

I took those lessons to heart and they became important tips for the year ahead. My relationship with Wardi also became a closer one. He was just as excited as I was whenever I was participating in races.

As much as I would love to have that kind of power in my legs, I swam with a six-beat kick just like the way he wanted. At times, it somehow lapsed back into my two-beat kick, out of tiredness from all that running and cycling.

After putting my best in all my training, I felt ready for the Metaman.

———◆———

The Metaman

After paying for the various races and expenditure that went into the sport of triathlon, Metaman looked like a pretty good deal with reasonable race entry fee, free carbo-loading lunch, fireworks, post-race buffet meal, swim recce, bike recce, run recce, good water, food and fuel support stations, pros autograph sessions (plus free poster given!), cheap ferry ticket and resort, and beach chill out areas. I could easily bring the bike up the ferry without wrapping it up, or placing it in a box. It sounded like an ideal race!

Here I was participating in my first half iron-distance triathlon, ready to take action on my very own Ironman dreams.

Metaman happened in August 2013 in Bintan Island, an island in the Riau Archipelago of Indonesia, an hour's ferry ride away from Singapore. The temperature was warm at about 32 degree Celsius with humidity at around 85 percent. It was the Hungry Ghost Festival month where some Chinese believed that spirits were out there in the waters, and posed threats to swimmers especially in the open waters. Other than this superstition, my menses actually came right on the day! I did not want to take any medication to alter my cycle, so I just needed to do what I needed to do and got prepared to make any change at the portable loos.

The day before the race was busy with registration, setting up the bike, testing the bike, transition bags and bike check-ins. At the registration area, I saw the real faces of these professionals --- some whom I had been watching on youtube videos - stood right in front of me. They were Chris McCormack, Belinda Granger, Guy Crawford, Dylan McNeice and several others. These people are real! Richard and I were busy identifying every professional out there. With a poster on hand, I was actually standing right next to these professionals.

The course for Metaman 70.3 took athletes on a spectacular journey around Bintan Island. With pool-like conditions in the swim, the ocean was clear and calm where many athletes completed the swim in a good time accompanied with some shower and pool of water to wash your sand off your feet. I completed my 1.9-kilometre swim in good time, much better than I usually would have done back then in the pool.

What was probably Kona-like was probably having someone passing us our transition bags, picking up our stuff, dropping our stuff back to the drop off point while we proceeded to get our bike. This was one of the rare chances of feeling like a pro in Kona, just like how I had viewed those youtube videos!

Although many athletes might say the 90.1-kilometre course in Bintan Island featured no big hills, they were definitely leg-sapping rolling roads and hills for an amateur like me for my first 70.3. As we approached the first hill out of the hotel, we knew that the entire 90.1 kilometres (that 0.1 kilometre still made a difference to me as an amateur!) would be hilly. In less than a kilometre, we were cycling out of our resort in a slope which was close to 15 percent grade climb. I could see a few athletes coming down from their bikes, and adjusting their bikes. With 10 kilometres out on the bike, first timers like me were beginning to feel the strain with hills of ranges of 10 to 20 percent grade.

As I rounded a corner and ascended a steep slope after 50-kilometre ride, I gave a shout out and went all out to climb that long steep hill, aided by a compact chainset and 11/28 cassette. A marshal rode past in his motorbike, and gave me a thumb up. Crosswinds and headwinds were blowing at athletes at about 10 kilometre per hour.

Climbing out of the shadows of our very own bikes up and down the killer hills of Bintan Island, it was like we had been transported to a similar challenge any hills would probably bring us. As the hot sun basked strongly on every athlete surrounded by the steep hills of Bintan, we were fortunate that the aid stations were filled with sufficient hydration, ice, gels and bananas. It was no wonder they called this the Killer Hills of Southeast Asia. The views were simply breathtaking.

At about noon when the sun was the hottest of up to about 35 degree Celsius with up to 90 percent humidity level, the road ahead dropped down to a sharp descent. I nicely controlled the smooth descent with cushioned low-vibration response amidst the slight shower just an hour ago.

On a particular hill, my right foot slipped from the pedal, and Milou was quick enough to respond to a halt when I held my brakes. As I cruised down the slopes, this guy came real fast, overtaking me at about 100 metres away from me.

Swoosh! He crashed as he came down the slope, with all the bike accessories falling all over the place.

I saw him slipping off from his bike down to the side of the road as he made a turn to the right. I was not too sure if he had lost control of his bike or the turn was just too sharp for him to maneuver. The race was not a full road-closed event, so I had to slow down to make sure that he was alright. By this point, a few athletes and volunteers had come over to ensure he was safe.

After cycling under the hot sun for hours, it was opportunistic to charge along with stability on the flatter terrains and shades near the beaches. I reminisced months ago when Richard and I were arguing over the material, weight and comfort of a saddle and we found saddle to be a very personal subject. The cushioned saddle of Milou did not have the coolest look but it had equipped me with sufficient comfort throughout the hills.

Whether it was a low-end aluminium bike or a high-end carbon triathlon bike, each of us had our very own. Everyone could identify the better climbers as we climbed those hills with whatever leg power we had left. For me, I just had to keep going.

It was technical and steep in some parts of the hills, and I felt I was going at a pace I was not sure I would be able to sustain for the day, but I had to try to keep up. As I made our final climb on the final hill, I saw a few cyclists getting off their bikes and pushing their bikes uphill. At this point, I could feel my legs starting to cramp any moment. I saw one athlete pushing his bike. His name was Joe, and this too was his first half-ironman distance triathlon race. I came down and we pushed our bikes a little before we continued our descent. I had to continue this journey as I had to keep the promise to my grandma who passed away not too long ago.

As we made a few more kilometres to the end of the bike leg, sudden exhilaration and voices rose among the athletes. All became a familiar sight of bells ringing, teams cheering and announcements being made clearer every kilometre. Many athletes got cramps on their legs as they dismounted from their bikes. Volunteers came forward, and helped me to rack my bike! These volunteers were simply marvelous!

At transition, I took a bite off my bread and continued my run. Three loops with a mix of slight slopes and shady trails around the resort - the run was not a walk in the park. While I could be enjoying the picturesque beachfront while running past the swimming pool, the sun above us shone strongly at our heads and back. For every second out there, I could feel my skin burning. At every aid station, there were carnages. I also saw a guy being stretched out. Athletes were grabbing every piece of hydration sponge, showering themselves with all the water they could get. I too showered myself and soaked myself with all the water there was. I also did not care whether I was having any overflow from my menses, and battled through the run leg. I just carried my bottle of water with me and sipped the water throughout the tough battlefields. While two Australian men who were pacing me and making their plans to make it to the finish line within the eight-hour mark, I too showed no signs of weakening. As I ran past the finish line which was 50 metres on my right, I signaled one more loop to the announcer. I started to feel excited, ran a faster run split, and completed the grueling Metaman 70.3 within the eight hours.

At the finish, I slowly enjoyed the buffet of pasta, pizzas, cakes, fruits, soup, bread, coke and drinks.

"We still have seven athletes out there", the announcement was made.

The athletes had 17 hours to complete the race. The sky had turned dark and Richard was still out there. I was patiently waiting. There he was, slowly jogging, walking and limping to the finish line. He too had finished his 70.3.

Just like running, I was glad we tried. I could have missed 100 percent of the shots that I might never take. If I were not even willing to try to make my dreams come true, I could have ended up settling for less of a life than I could have had. I would still be grumbling about the woes and pains of working life and perhaps still sitting down in that coach thinking what I should be eating for my next meal to lose that bit of calories off my body.

Chapter 13

More than we had Bargained for

Somewhere in between the extremes of triathlon and work lies a reasonable balance. I knew that with the effort I had put in, I could achieve such great goals; but I also knew that there was more to life than just my career and my sport. Everyone has different talents, with some incredibly talented and capable people out there from all walks of life.

Although good luck was not exactly part of my skillset as yet, I welcomed them as they helped me accomplish things.

I received a phone call from the press one morning. I was chosen to join a sprint cycling trial along the F1 racing tracks with Robbie McEwen, a triple winner in the Tour de France. Along with the lucky few who were selected for this sprint, we took our road bikes to the test with two laps of 5.05- kilometre of the Singapore F1 Race Course. We had the entire F1 course to ourselves with no traffic at all. Humble as we cycled on the course, we could feel how fast these F1 drivers drove along the course. We also received awesome cheers from supporters and fantastic food spread and chats with Robbie. Robbie was an amicable star as he shared his experiences with us.

❖

To me in triathlon, it was not about winning or losing. Moving ahead in my life now, I did not want to look backwards in life years from now, filled with regrets, disappointments or negative emotions in life.

After every race, Richard and I reviewed my performance from a scale of one to ten and I would often give a loose figure of an average of five to seven. When I finished my Metaman, I felt a definite ten that I could go for the full iron-distance triathlon.

I looked at my calendar, and I had a few months window period in the beginning of first half of the year. It was a choice between Challenge Taiwan and Ironman Port Macquarie. In terms of history, Challenge Taiwan was newer than Port Macquarie. There was also limited information on Challenge Taiwan.

While there was a big deal to some professional triathletes in distinguishing Challenge and Ironman races, I felt it was a brand game, and there wasn't any difference in the distances. Both races posed similar challenges on the swim, bike and run course - lake versus port waters conditions, undulating versus some steep gradients of the bike courses, and various terrains for the runs.

Just like marathons and half-iron distance triathlons, there were pesky things called time cutoffs for full iron-distance triathlon. In other words, I could not take a few days to complete the race. I could still force my way through to continue the race once the sweeper come and take me off the course, but I am officially still a DNF (which meant Did Not Finish). The 3.8-kilometre swim cutoff was two hours twenty minutes, the 180-kilometre bike to be completed by 10.5 hours, and 17 hours by the time I finished my 42-kilometre marathon. The cut-off times were the same for both male and female athletes. In fact, in some races, the cut-off times were even shorter!

Logistically it appeared Taiwan was more of a nightmare for us, having to travel from one airport or bus terminal to another. While I was still contemplating, the "registration" button was staring right in front of me. I did not get myself to push that little rectangular "confirm" button that gave me the opportunity to conquer 226 kilometres and 17 hours out there on a course just because I thought I had what it takes. A time cut-off of 17 hours --- anyone could have slept half the day, washed the dishes, ironed the clothes, probably had lunch with friends or went out shopping, and even finished watching a movie. There was no guarantee that I could finish the race. But to literally sit on my bed and witness pure marvelousness on the sheer determination of every athlete out there each time I watch the video, it was utterly spectacular how such sport triggered that kind of emotions that filled my eyes with tears. It was somehow more than just a check off the bucket list. I went ahead and pressed the button.

Later that night I was lying awake for a long time worrying about how I could ever finish this race. The longest ride I had ever done so far was the 100 kilometres in Iskandar Malaysia, and I almost felt like dying from it.

In the months leading up to the race, Richard and I started to put some structure to our training ahead, targeting some of the major "B" and "C" events. To be in absolute peak condition, I could not train hard all year round, so we also planned switching to less and more laid-back training til my "A" race.

Richard wanted the best out of me, and I could not deny him that chance. We discovered the special activity that Richard and I could do together – building up our bicycles and parts in an exercise book, replenishing the supply of gels, hydration and supplements, monitoring and developing our training plans together.

Hong Kong

Things sure had their own way of turning out. Richard chanced upon Hong Kong ITU Olympic Distance Triathlon race during my birthday week. It might be an ITU level race but it was open for the public to register.

My relatives in Hong Kong were always close to my heart. They had helped me in my triathlon journey – resolving my logistical challenges to and from race site, hotel and airport.

I received much confusion over miscommunication of information from the organiser. For hours, we scrambled like headless chickens from one end of the island to the other, leaving us to get to the race pack collection at very late hours.

On race day morning, it was cold at about 19 degree Celsius. With a torch on hand, I made my way around the transition area. I looked around and checked with the volunteers about the swim and bike exit. It was a wrong move. They were not familiar. In any way, I got myself ready and walked a long stretch of about 500m to the platform.

It was my first platform swim start. And it was not a wet suit swim. Despite some currents in the waters around the pier, I completed the single loop swim, and ran to the transition 500-metre away. With the race site around Disneyland area, the bike route took athletes through the strong headwinds and highways. Traffic near Disneyland compound was not well managed as several accidents happened. I was riding slower than usual, so I gave my thanks to God for my safe return and I proceeded to my run. The looped run leg was held under the sun in the open fields with no isotonic drinks at the aid stations. While medals, finisher tees and towels were distributed to finishers, the race was not spectator-friendly as Richard could not access many areas. Soon, I too joined the finishers and completed this ITU race.

Did you know?

> *Practise all forms of swim start. I placed my chins down before I made the plunge at the platform to prevent waters from getting into my googles.*

> *Many people in Hong Kong did not know where or how to book a vehicle which would be large enough to carry my bike. Most budget hotels would claim there are no such resources. It could cost up to about HKD$500 to book a van (at least 24 hours in advance) which could logistically carry your bike to your desired site.*

I was running in the run leg of the ITU Hong Kong Triathlon.

Malaysia

Names of triathlon races vary from countries to countries, though they might sound the same. A friend actually mistook "Nusajaya Triathlon" in Malaysia, as "Noosa Triathlon" in Australia.

Nusajaya Triathlon, a slightly longer than Olympic Distance Triathlon, was happening in Johor Bahru, Malaysia. It was organised by a long-time veteran triathlete, Uncle Chan. Uncle Chan was a knowledgeable veteran who never stopped to mentor and guide triathletes.

Johor Bahru is about 30 kilometres from Singapore. It might look near to Singapore, but it had given me quite a hell of an adventure cycling through the narrow lanes and heavy traffic at Woodlands Immigration Checkpoint in Singapore before we even reached the bridge linking between Singapore and Johor Bahru. Uncle Chan was waiting to pick us up on the other side of the bridge at Johor Bahru. He took care of all of us despite only four out of ten actually turned up at the meeting venue.

Swimming in the Puteri Harbour was nice with calm (but oily unclear and at some points underwater currents) waters. While being hit by breaststrokers, I also dealt with several sea bugs and cold currents in the waters. I swam according to plan and took extra care on the run along the slippery route to the transition.

As typical rustic Malaysia roads, the bike ride took athletes along the scenic roads of Nusajaya. With head winds, I paddled along the roads with some gravels at times, up the mild slopes of Nusajaya highways and immersed myself in this adventure. My legs were feeling great, with no signs of cramps or whatsoever. Richard who joined me in this race had a flat tyre though.

I mounted my bike, dumped my bike stuff and put on my gear for the run. At noon, the temperature rose to 34 degree Celsius. While the run course which took part of the cycling course was relatively flat, my heart rate was still shooting upwards as I ran. It slowed to a walk while I poured water over myself at every water station. Sheer focus on breathing and running made me finish the race with a negative split. Overall, it was a well-organised race. The race just revealed my weak mental strength under the heat.

Did you know?

> *Logistically, it would be easier if we had rented a car, put our stuff into the car and drive across the checkpoint than to ride across dangerously.*

> *Just like Iskandar Malaysia, the town was so new that the location did not appear in our GPS devices.*

Cambodia

Our decision to visit Siem Reap was not an immediate one. Rather than to participate in Singapore marathon which was held on the same day, we decided to visit Ang Kor Wat, a UNESCO site with its beauty and state of preservation and joined their half marathon in 2013.

Since we were already at Ang Kor Wat, we also signed up for 100-kilometre Bike4Kids charity ride which was held a day earlier than the half marathon. Ang Kor Wat Bike4Kids 100-kilometre Charity Ride was a race and fight against exploitation of childen in Cambodia. It was a ride of four loops around the archaeological sites and temples of Ang Kor. On race day, we rented our mountain bikes and cycled through the dark roads to the race site. I could always remember not replacing my lights with new batteries and having to ride through total darkness to the race start.

Because of the vastness of about 400 square kilometres, the plan of Ang Kor Wat was difficult to grasp. I was so lost that I made the same turn twice around a temple. Along the way, I admired the architecture. These stones were beautifully elevated into towers, chambers, porches, courtyards and even stairways. The finishing ride culminated back to the decorated start point. I completed my first 100-kilometre ride on a mountain bike at an average speed of about 22 kilometres per hour. I guessed this was not too bad for my first ride on a mountain bike for that distance.

The next day, Ang Kor Wat Half Marathon took us around the Ang Kor Wat UNESCO site again, this time on foot. In a race organised by a Third World country like Cambodia, we did not expect much. We were grateful that the carbo-loading party was filled with a range of Khmer food.

I was taking a quick picture while running the Siem Reap Half Marathon.

The race route was impressive, allowing us to run through the magnificent remains of the Khmer Empire, Temples and countless sculptures, while we took lots of pictures along the way. We finished in less than 3 hours, but the organiser had run out of medals. We suspected the street kids would have taken most of them.

A trip would not be completed without finishing off with another bike trip up Beng Mealea.

Beng Mealea or Bung Mealea is a temple in the Ang Kor Wat style located 40 kilometres east of the main group of temples at Ang Kor, Cambodia, on the ancient royal highway to Preah Khan Kompong Svay. As we pedaled with a higher cadence up the slopes on our way to the temple amidst the sandy or muddy trails and roads, we enjoyed our ride filled with meals, fruits, and educational information about their culture.

Did you know?

> *An interesting fact was we did not bring our bicycle to the race. We brought our own clip-on pedals. I had to ask for the smallest bike and fit my pedals onto the bike for a more comfortable ride.*

> *There was no taxi in Siem Reap, so it was easy to lift our bikes onto the tuk tuk.*

> *Bringing own lights for such rides was helpful in lighting our paths to the race site. Ensure sufficient battery though!*

Australia

Amidst our regular weekly training rides and races of both intervals and longer ones, our rides never get longer than 100 kilometres. It was just about less than three months away from my "A" race --- Challenge

Taiwan full iron-distance triathlon. If there were ways to address issues around confidence, motivation, anxiety or fear, they had to be addressed right now. Signing up for a 70.3 was one possible way.

Geelong with its beautifully placed waterfront views presented athletes with calm waters and multi-looped fast course. The run terrains were pretty steep of about 15 percent grade. Having trained in Bintan, and running the MacRitchie hills in Singapore, I knew I could do this. The cut-off was 7.5 hours, which could be a little challenging for me. I guessed challenges were what made our lives interesting. I decided to give it a shot.

With a water temperature of 15 degree Celsius, Geelong would be my first wet suit race. I had swum with the wet suit when I was training back in Singapore. The feeling of sticking your body into a heavy rubber piece of material irked me, let alone the fuss of putting them through my body.

"Sigh!" I sighed in frustration as I just finished putting both legs through.

Richard smiled at me, and knew that I had to do this myself.

"Slowly", he repeated.

In a tropical country like Singapore, we never get to use the wet suits at all. After a 20-minute effort of putting it on, I felt I was like one of the superhero characters in a skintight suit, and I could hardly breathe. When I tried to swim in the cold waters of Geelong a day before race day, I was still feeling uncomfortable. Days before race day, Richard and I shopped around the race site, and we managed to buy a lighter wet suit at a very good price.

The race entry did not include a carbo-loading dinner, so I had my quick dinner with Richard at a nearby restaurant and turned in early.

These were the nights where I lied on the bed, tossing and turning. With the outside breeze going strong at about 16 degree Celsius late at night, I found my imagination going wild and I was unsure if I could complete the race. I was also still hesitating over which wetsuit I should be using for the race.

On race morning, I woke up and picked the lighter wetsuit. As I was placing my water bottles onto my bike, my neighbouring athlete asked me if I was a good swimmer. I understood her totally when I saw the waters that day. The winds were hammering, and there was quite a huge bit of wind chop on the swim course.

As I looked around, everyone was bigger than me. The next few minutes were a panicked blur of athletes, while I sent endless mobile messages to my swimming coach and taking deep breaths to calm myself down. Clenching my fist while waiting for my swim start, I looked up and in front of me reflected a dark grey sky amidst the rough waters. There were no birds singing among the sombre sky. There was also not a sight of fish in the waters. I felt conflicted over the peaceful scene the day before the race day. Amidst the darkness I also started to feel an unknown fear of the unseen and toothsome creatures that made their home out there in the salty open waters.

As it was all dark, I still went ahead and did my short warm-up of about 50 metres out. The warm-up felt deceivingly doable. I could not visualise how I would be swimming around the markers. I just knew I had to swim back to shore before time cut-off.

Unlike other races, I could not see Richard before I dived in when the horn sounded off. An all-out running sprint into the water sent my heart rate skyrocketing.

The reality then set in. Below the sea surface, it was rough and dark. The cool water seeped into my wetsuit as I stroked out towards the marker post. When I was swimming 200 metres out towards the post, I realised that the waves just got larger and stronger. They came up to a couple of metres above me.

By the time I started swimming, I was so panic-stricken and desperate for escape that I had no concept of race pace. I just swam as hard as I could until the nightmare was over. I switched from front crawl to breaststroke. A menacing blare pierced my senses, and it took all my will to keep swimming. All I knew was I just aimed to finish the swim by swimming one marker at a time. After about 15 minutes, I still could not sight the first marker! Everyone was swimming faster than me.

The gap increased: 20 metres became 50 metres, and 50 metres then became 100 metres. Before I knew, I could hardly identify any athletes in front of me. I stopped, looked around and then realised I could see no one. Before I knew it, the next sea wave hit me. The next wave of swimmers was coming up. *Just keep going.*

What was worse was that I started to get dizzy and nauseas. I was bobbing up and down. For that moment, I was thinking if this would be how I would be dying. There were no canoes near me. I felt miserable. I had not even said a good bye to Richard.

During this process, a sudden feeling and sense of calmness overwhelmed me. I could only do what I could do. I closed my eyes, took three further deep breaths and kept reminding myself to relax. It did not matter if there was finesse to a swim like this. It descended to a struggle for survival.

I raised my arm and shouted for help. The stronger swimmers came and asked if I was alright. I was treading water. Such were the wonders of the camaraderie of the triathlon sport.

Nevertheless, I continued my race. I needed the experience of a race before my full iron-distance triathlon. I took some time to calm myself before I continued onto my bike leg. I heaved a sigh of relief as I had earlier put my chain at a gear ratio of which I could jump onto my bike immediately and pedal at a comfortable speed of up to 26 kilometres per hour, before climbing the 20 percent gradient slope 50 metres in front of the bike exit. As I was slowly grinding up the slope, a couple of guys cycled past me in a breeze. They looked like they had plenty of gas!

The cool temperature of 15 degree Celsius in the morning had by then started to rise to about 36 degree Celsius. The heat was not a big deal. It was the wind that destroyed the motivation and enthusiasm of many athletes. On the bike leg, the winds got up to about 50 kilometres per hour with gusts of up to about 70 kilometres per hours.

With the slight tail wind, we were cruising along the highway at 50 kilometres per hour. After 30 kilometres, the trip back was extremely tough as I crawled under 15 kilometres per hour, and felt like I was barely moving. As I saw the bikes in front of me swaying side to side, I had Milou starting to move just like them.

With a few twists and turns through the park, two hills and some elevations of about 400 metres, the bike course was not exactly a scenic one with the road surface consisting of a mix of rough surfaces and pot holes. I enjoyed cycling on the roads through the Eastern Park and Esplanade with supporters cheering for us. As I cycled close to the end of the bike course, I overheard that a portion of the bike course was closed off for about 30 minutes due to the danger caused by the strong windstorms.

After I was done on the bike, I continued on the run. Every athlete's face showed the fatigue and the disappointment. Everyone was just not feeling great.

Strong winds continued for the day. First time ever, I saw athletes drafting one another on the run. Caps, cups, race belts, gels and plastic bags were blown all over the place. It was simply a big mess all over the grounds. I eventually finished the run in slightly less than three hours. It was an extremely tough day out, and it definitely had put me in a stronger mental preparation for the races ahead.

As I sat down and had my late lunch with Richard, I saw a scene across the bar top table.

A lady shrugged off her friend, as her friend comforted her, "I could give you my medal."

"I don't want your medal." I overhead a scathing reply.

Her friend was trying to explain how tough the race was, and even for those strong athletes who completed, they failed to complete the race in good time.

The point was the friend did not finish.

That scene reminded me of how fragile human beings could be, such that when a person valued something in her life, she would raise her expectations on it, cherish it, and protect it. I too had cried over a race in the past because of a disappointment that I had placed so much hope upon.

I finished that last bit of fish on my plate, and reflected on my performance for the race.

I had my dream, and I followed the path I thought I would enjoy. While I might have prepared myself for every condition in a race, I could never prepare for the unexpected. It was a hard day for everyone that day.

While the physical challenge was probably not that significant, this race mentally threw every athlete out. How often had we been critical to ourselves such that we think we just could not handle the stress anymore? We often make a choice based on what we see, and how we feel at the time. And based on that, we make the call, and move on in life. I might not be able to predict or control the weather, but I knew I could control how I felt against the nasty weather. There was no failure for anyone, except our failure to learn.

Did you know?

> *There were Australian triathlon races with non-numbered racks at the transition area. This meant whoever reached first would probably get the best position he identified. It was crucial to pick the right gear on the cassette of my bike before racking my bike. This could help me to ride my bike smoothly the moment I mount onto my bike.*

Batam

Two months before my "A" race, a friend from the triathlon community invited me to join the inaugural Batam Olympic Distance Triathlon, a late addition to the race calendar. This sounded like a nice refresher for my Challenge Taiwan.

Aside from Bintan, Batam is the other large island in the Riau Islands Province of Indonesia, an hour ferry ride away from Singapore. A bus then took us from the ferry terminal to our resort. Although the stretch was picturesque, the roads were filled with cars, trucks, buses and motorbikes. While the bus broke into a slow trotting climb, every athlete in the bus sat up straight and looked ahead on the hilly bike terrain. We could hear the gearing of the bus as it dragged up the slopes. The silence in the bus broke into an atmosphere of anxiety and strategic planning of how the various athletes would be climbing up the slopes on race day. The race was located at a resort, which helped families and athletes to spend more time together and yet allowed athletes to focus on their rest for race day.

On Sunday, my alarm on my handphone burst into life an hour earlier. It was five in the morning. The black coffee in the resort failed to jolt me while my stomach was still heaving with a few slices of bread filled with peanut butter.

The sun had risen and the adventure had begun. The swim brought athletes swimming not more than 10 metres away from the luxurious huge yauchts berthed at the marina. Caution was taken in keeping a safe distance from them. I just could not imagine my arms flinging onto these yauchts. The cost of scratching or damaging them would probably be higher than injuring my own arms.

After making my swim exit, I faced an immediate long steep slope of at least 15 percent gradient, leading all the way to the entrance of the resort of less than a kilometre away. With my bike on the small chain wheel on a light gear, I took a deep breath before I sprinted with almost full gas for as long as I could hold, spinning the pedals, and powering myself to the top. As I cycled through the long sections of lush green vegetation, the longer I rode along the hills and highways, the route exposed me to more bare and red clayey landscape. The hills were not longer than three kilometres but they were definitely steep of about 15 percent gradient or even more.

After cycling for about 15 kilometres, I slowed down to flick down my gears. My cadence was dropping, my legs were burning, my heart was beating hard, and I was still gasping for air as I cycled my way up. I could not find any lighter gears on my bike. It was just my legs and my bike now. Finally I reached the top of a hill. As I reached for a drink on my bike, another climb came into view. I was sure it was steeper than the earlier one.

While going up and down the bridge did bring a certain fulfillment to the athletes, care and caution pursued as we negotiated our way back onto the chaotic roads of Batam again on our last part of our ride back. There was no signage, and I was totally dependent on the marshals. Every hill I faced was a challenge I gave myself to complete.

With about 10 kilometres more to go, I made a turn to the left, and it brought me back to the bike start line again. I could not help but noticed the weary expressions of the faces of the triathletes as they rode past me. With the sun shining at me, and the temperatures hitting 36 degrees Celsius, the announcer asked me if I had made a second loop.

"What second loop?" I asked.

I realised that I should have turned to the right, but the marshal directed me to the wrong route! It was an extra few kilometres of hard hills I climbed!

I had no time to think, and I just kept going.

Making a quick change at the transition, I made for the run at the undulating hill terrains of the golf course. There was absolutely no shelter, no wind, but just sealed cups of mineral water at the aid stations.

At average of less than 9 minutes per kilometre pace, I was going at a really slow pace, afraid of a cramp coming up. As I looked across, I could feel every triathlete dragging their feet along to the finish. I was definitely not the only one suffering. As I made my last climb up, I ran faster and faster for the final few hundred metres to the finish. Running around a golf course was much tougher than I had thought!

Fluids and nutrition helped athletes replenish the huge amounts of sweat loss under the scorching weather. No one mentioned about PB. Under the hellish condition, I was thankful that I did not suffer any cramps.

I ran the golf course under the immense heat of Batam.

With the pool less than 50 metres away, I dived in and cooled myself crazy while I waited for Richard to finish his race.

While I was chilling out, my friend shouted for me. The eyes of the triathletes descended upon me; photographers swooped down armed with cameras, all wanting an account of the winners. This was my first podium win in a triathlon. I got third. Aside from the cash prize, I also had a good pick of choices of bike components from a cardboard box. I was privileged to receive the bronze medal specially brought over by a group of officers from the Komodo Multilateral Naval Exercise 2014.

Did you know?

> *Richard pushed himself to the finishing line when the volunteers started to keep the medals and clear the table.*

> *We joined this triathlon with a mindset to win, that is, we will not give up and we will not lose.*

> *Just like I carry this mindset in my job, this game or this sport, I do not believe in not performing too bad and survive the day as it comes. I will not gain anything and in fact I am losing everything – my time, my effort and my potential.*

Part 3
Embracing Life

Chapter 14

Allied Voices, My Voice

Training for a Full Iron Distance Triathlon

Signing up for a full iron-distance triathlon was a fairly bittersweet endeavor for me. It felt sweet because what I had been watching on the youtube was coming true for me. This big dream - I conjured up with Chris when we were having coffee in a cafe a few years ago - was smacking right in my face. However it was just as bitter because with my state I was in coupling with all the stresses at work or with my family, I knew I had to manage this immense heat coming to me.

With triathlon in your life, it could make or break your relationship with your loved ones. Other than growing up from our families of different backgrounds and stories, we faced family issues, shouldering the responsibility of a leader and managing teams at work, and handling midlife career crisis --- all of which were just the beginning. Listening to the stories of my sick and ailing grandparents, my stubborn parent, my forgetful siblings or my broken body, handling difficulties in my jobs or whatever else life dished out and came along --- these were not going to be over in a hurry.

My dad told me I was no athlete, and that sports would be useless for me. My mum told me that sports would endanger my life. I had many other friends who felt that the sport was too time-consuming. The bike retailers told me I was too short and would not be easy to get a bike for my size. My *shifu* felt that I should not exert myself on endurance exercises if they were giving me gastrointestinal and difficulty in breathing issues. What the future lies ahead, I do not know. I just keep learning and improving myself.

All these were playing in my head over and over again.

It looked like there will be some things we cannot help and there are things we cannot change.

Life would be what we chose to make out of it. I had a six-month window period of which I needed some form of aim or personal achievements in life. It got a little more challenging when uncertainty crept in at work. I had gone this far, and I was thriving off my past challenges and goals.

I must *now* step up.

Other than dedicating the full iron-distance triathlon to my dear ones who had left me, the race was specifically dedicated to me - recognising how far I had come and how much more I could give. Somehow within me, the youtube videos were still playing in my head. The same set of questions came to me. How could these people with physical disabilities, some probably with worse problems than those of mine could actually finish their race within the 17 hours cut-off? More importantly, why would they do that?

I was ready to open my mind and learn to see this world of *the* Ironman.

Along with such great aspirations, I was blessed with the love of Richard and his family. His family lived in Ipoh, Malaysia. Richard and I would take time to visit them once every few months. Time spent with his family was invigorating. They eat simple meals like rice, vegetable, meat dishes, and fruits. They have differences in opinions and raise voices with one another but they respect one another, and cheer one another with bowls of noodles or cups of coffee after that. The care, love and support provided by Richard's family touched me deeply.

I raced on a foldie (bought from a shop recommended by Richard's father) in a night race in Ipoh, Malaysia.

The way I was brought up in my family, the loss of my dear ones in my life, and the many opportunities I had lost since childhood – these had definitely left an indelible mark in my mind. Now I recognised them, I wanted to convince people beyond these scars and let them know me as who I really am – the girl who always pursue excellence in life.

If I had made it through the series of adversities clinging to my life, just how tough could this full iron-distance triathlon be? I wanted to redefine what was possible.

The greatest challenge for me in completing a full iron-distance triathlon was the long bike course. This meant I needed to build up my endurance for the distance, spend quite a couple of hours daily, and almost half a day on my bike during weekends. So daily, I started my training with an hour on the stationary bike, and another hour of running after work. At the end of the day, I was totally beaten.

On certain weekends when I joined certain cycling or triathlon races, I faced one common question, "Which cycling group do you belong to?"

In a busy city like Singapore, most cyclists join cycling groups, and they cycle at night. Some cyclists like the fun, and benefits of cycling in a draft-friendly group. While some cyclists gear towards the recreational side, there are some who go for the more serious affair. When I first started joining the group rides, I remembered vividly I was one of the last cyclists, as a female cyclist. I also had plenty of opportunities in having a grueling hill workout, tempo cycling, and leg-searing lactate threshold sessions.

"What do you think about Tour de Bintan?" I asked the leader of M Riders.

He laughed, and asked me not to even think about it. Other than having hesitation on cycling on roads with low visibility at nights, I also had my reservations of continuing with these cycling groups with cyclists who were just too snobbish as if they were the only ones who knew about cycling.

Soon, I started a group ride of my own of some sorts --- short, sharp, and focused. I did not just train with my usual old friends; instead I trained alone more often. Instead of the gossipy scene of group rides or group runs, I was focusing on my own numbers, and my own goals.

In the months leading to Challenge Taiwan, I trained even harder than before, and joined races across multiple disciplines. Despite a few adjustments to my bike, I still did not feel comfortable. After hearing of the different bike fits conducted by retailers, self-proclaimed bike fitters and training coaches, I approached my professional Retul trained bike fitter, Choonwei for help.

With all the sensor stickers and wires placed on my joints and contact points, I cycled on the turbo trainer, as the system measured the average of all my angles. Choonwei then made several adjustments which included saddle, handle bar heights, and position. Although the Retul bike fit cost me a hefty S$550, I received a report of all my bike measurements, and felt comfortable after that. This was my best purchase to date.

This was the place where I had my bike fit.

One year after our first half iron-distance triathlon, Richard and I were ready to fly to Taitung, Taiwan. Chris, my supporter also came along with us. Racing around the world sounded like a pretty cool idea, but the logistical fuss of bike travel snapped us back to reality, especially when we were already tight on budget travel. We would be charged extra if we exceeded the weight limit after we had checked in our 20-kilogram bike boxes and race essentials.

Upon arrival at Taitung Airport, we asked around for directions, but no one seemed to know about the race event. The airport logistics who were supposed to transport our bikes were also not kept informed, and left our bike boxes stranded on the carpark grounds.

Knowing we had to go through several transits, we arrived in Taitung a few days earlier to acclimate and adjust to the environment. We played tourist, settled in, and adjusted to the climate as it grew hotter each day.

Staying in a double-storey shophouse helped. The owner supported us in every way he could – transporting the bikes from airport to race sites, lending us commuter bikes to move around, showing us the cheap and good food around the place, and making healthy sandwiches and fruit juice every day.

When we showed up at the race expo for our race pack collection, my meeting with the professional triathletes helped to calm my nerves. Belinda Granger, one of the elites, who has been in this sport for years, shared her enthusiasm and encouragement.

"This is a perfect race for first timers. If you have done Bintan, this is nothing", Belinda shared.

Of course this was nothing to her – an elite professional!

That sure was a big boost of confidence for me.

That evening, we went for our carbo-loading party, which was a similar simple affair as the race expo. With the race briefing explained in both English and Mandarin, we were prepared for a good race ahead.

Chapter 15

Completing the Full Iron-Distance Triathlon

April 25, 2014 was a beautiful day in Taitung in southeast Taiwan. It was cool at about 23 degree Celsius. The race had been known to be quite a spectacular - range of mountains mixed with a pristine tropical coastline lined with farms, rice fields and villages. The race was also set to be a personal battle to break away from all fears and past history, and to emerge with a triumph. The full iron-distance triathlon was set to begin first thing that morning.

My energy, heart, and soul had been poured into training for this "A" race. Richard and I wanted to show up on the starting line knowing that we did everything we could to the best of our capabilities to prepare for this race. The months of training leading to this "A" race were undoubtedly demanding in terms of cost, time, energy, and commitment. There was no turning back.

On race day, a sense of calmness overwhelmed me. Richard and I went about our usual routine of taking our breakfast early. As we had racked up our bikes the day before, the owner was kind enough to wake up early and send us to the race site in his car. Arriving two hours earlier at the race site, I had some time to make another trip to the toilet. I checked and rechecked my bike for the right tyre pressure, speedometer, nutrition, and hydration. I had a final check of the items in my drop-in bag before I handed the bag to the truck. Athletes wished one another well, and gathered at the swim platform. At this time, we heard about the professional triathlete, Chris McCormack looking for another pair of goggles as his goggles had broken.

We made our way through the crowd to the swim platform. Richard's uncontrollable habit of putting his protruding ears tucked under his swimming cap with his small little eyes gazing at me gave me a laugh.

"Remember to keep going, no matter what it takes", I told Richard. Richard laughed and said that he would make it as far as the official would allow him.

With the morning sunrise, I stood at the swim platform and felt good to go. The waters was 23 degree Celsius. It was a wetsuit swim. I popped in a salt tablet. These salt tablets are sodium- and electrolyte-replacement supplements which I often take to replenish the salt lost through perspiration.

Time passed quickly during pre-race. The professionals had gone off, and soon it was our turn. The swim was two loops around the lake. We felt weird seeing a whole bunch of athletes crowding at a distance away from the u-turn point. We stayed clear of the hundreds of other athletes by locating ourselves at optimal positions at the swim platform.

Then the cannon fired, and we were off to our race. We had 2 hours and 20 minutes to complete the swim course. I dived into the lake from the platform. The swimming experience I had from Hong Kong Triathlon helped. The waters were calm with some underwater currents. The lifeguards and canoes followed closely while we swam along the length of the lake.

The first loop was easy. It was still a stretch. I could hardly see the last buoy before I could make my turn. As I swam, I saw quite a couple of swimmers without wet suits. Their braving the cold temperatures of the waters amazed me. After the u-turn back, I felt the lake was indeed long. I was still moving forward, so I had to be patient with the swim. I was cautious of cramps, and tried not to kick too hard.

Look at those canoes and lifeguards, so close to us, watching over us! Feeling safe, I found a groove and comfort zone, as I breathed on my right, stroked, breathed on the left, and stroked. These became the basic process of finishing my two loops. After making that turn, I increased my pace of swim. I could see one of the blue cappers following a relay swimmer.

Why is this chap going that way? You are off, man!

Nevertheless, I kept focused on swimming straight. On my way back after my second lap, I was sprinting on my last 100 metres. My heart was pumping faster and faster. I was not very far off from the rest of the pack. I felt calm and swam to the swim finish. The volunteers were helpful, and helped swimmers out of the slippery floors.

One done, two more to go.

The atmosphere was cool with all the excitement and yelling. As I ran up the 200-metre slope towards the transition zone, I felt as if I knew all the supporters as they were cheering for me.

Smile, Sof, smile!

I looked to the left and to the right, and waved at them. They did not know who I was, but I was drawing every form of positivity I could get to keep me going. The pace through the first transition was hot as I could see the split between the slower swimmers and the faster cyclists. I walked briskly to the transition area. While trying to remove my wet suit and running along the designated path, I ran past my transition bag, and had to go back a little. I was calm.

Still.

I grabbed my bag and made my way on the side to take off my swimming cap, goggles, and my wet suit entirely. While I put on my cycling gear and all, I was relieved to see so many people still putting on their gear. I had a quick bite on a piece of peanut butter sandwich before picking up my bike and off I went.

The bike course in Taitung was unlike the roads of Singapore. The lanes went in opposite direction. This meant we had to ride on the right side of the roads. The bike course was undulating and not flat. And they were not totally closed. It was a simple two-loop out-and-back course, so I broke down into quarters to make them more manageable in my mind. For each long stretch, I had them dedicated to a dear one I loved. The early loop was entertaining as I watched the professional athletes passed us at least twice.

I was pretty concerned about the 180-kilometre bike course as I had never done an entire 180 kilometres before. I had neither a triathlon bike nor aero-bars on my bike. Milou was all I got. Out on the first loop, I felt I could manage the terrain, and it boded well. If I could keep to that pace of average 25 kilometres per hour, which I felt it was possible at that point, I would be on track. I cautioned myself it was still early in the race, along with the cool temperature and still going strong body.

Focus. Focus. Focus.

Right at this moment, I was going uphill. Fortunately, it was a turnaround after this hill. I could see it. I had to lie to my brain to keep myself going.

My special needs bag was just less than two kilometres away. I had all my nutrition and additional aid in there - milo, isotonic, coke, bread, Pringles, socks, cannister, extra tube. I looked at my speedometer --- still keeping to my strategy of going an average of 24 to 26 kilometres per hour.

On my return route, there was barely any athlete left on the course. I had to dig deep and stay focused.

You are going to make it. It is only one last stretch, Sof. You can do this.

Despite the availability of marshals at certain points, I chanced upon two close dangerous encounters down when I was cycling at only 25 kilometres per hour! The policeman at a junction near the bridge area was not doing his duty at all. The car driving out from the side of the road almost moved out into my lane. I held my brakes a couple of times. The other time was when I was on my way back to town, a stalled motorbike suddenly turned left without looking on the rider's left. I had to shout out loud. There just were not enough marshals on the entire route. While the drafting rules stood, athletes were drafting like crazy!

As I rode and turned for my second loop on the bike course, I saw Richard on the other side. He signaled to me to keep focus and move on. He still had a stretch to go. I guessed that he might not make it to the bike cut-off. For a moment, this was a difficult choice I had to make. Should I stop the race and join him or do I keep moving forward?

Into my second loop on the bike course, the winds started to pick up along with some heat and traffic. While the breeze was largely welcomed as a cooling relief to athletes, the headwinds increased in intensity on the return laps. My speed dropped to less than 23 kilometres per hour. The last 40 kilometres seemed to last forever! All these heightened traffic suddenly was impacting my ride.

A voice came to my mind. That moment, I cycled as fast as I could. Emotions got over me. I stopped looking at my watch.

Come on! Forget about the distance. Take a look around you. Everyone else is going through the same thing as you. Look at their faces!

As the athletes made a turn back on the bike course, I had a good look at their faces. They were not grimacing at all.

They must be working harder than you, you slacker!

I flogged myself. In set intervals of 40 seconds, I went all out. As I could feel the perspiration rolling down my face and chin, I told myself that the water seeping from my pores could never match those tears that came from my eyes months ago. Wrapped up among the faster athletes, I savored every metre I rode on the bike course, with every sense being on alert mode.

You have gone through the worst in life...you can do this.

Intervals by intervals, I was climbing my way up. The views indeed were astounding with rugged mountains meeting the sea just like those pictures I saw in the postcards.

The aid station volunteers were trained and taught where and how to pass the bike bottles to us as we cruised down the lanes. With their over-enthusiastic attitude, I was totally soaked in their energy and cheers. For that moment, I forgot about my stress. After a steep stretch, one of the Taiwanese athletes cycled side-to-side with me.

"Where are you from?" he shouted as he cycled along with me.

"Singapore!" I shouted as I continued to cycle.

"Welcome to Taiwan!" he grinned with a grimace. The Taiwanese athlete was amazed with how I could cycle up the slope while sitting on the saddle.

I was cycling feeling happier each passing minute. Amidst our pain, we laughed. The cool temperature definitely helped lessen the aches in me.

I told myself I must make it. I had made too many sacrifices for this race.

This was it. *The Ironman. This was what you had asked for, Sof.*

Thirty-five minutes later, tearing away and muscles feeling still good, I knew I could finish my bike course. I saw a few athletes stopping by the side probably to walk off the cramps. I was just cycling at a comfortable speed, and not rushing to get any faster to prevent my legs from cramping up.

As we approached the bike finish, the volunteers were cheering for us and shouted, "Pang!" This meant *Good Job* in Chinese.

As I dismounted from my bike, I savoured every minute of that feeling. It was one of the most incredible moments. I actually finished a 180-kilometre bike ride. That would be something that probably last me a long time.

That made two of us. Richard too did finish his bike course, though about 15 minutes off the bike cut-off. But the fact was Richard finished the 180 kilometres.

I could see the many bikes which had been racked up. I was not done. I needed to finish a 42 kilometre run to finish this race.

Hurting. Heart was pounding.

I could feel my right feet in pain due to the constant hard pedaling. As I sat down to change my shoes, I could feel a sharp twinge of pain beneath the cleats of my shoes. I was careful in my seating position. How I sat on the ground could result in further cramps. Extra hydration, salts, nutrition and aid items were all in my transition bag. But for that few minutes of lethargy and while trying to catch my breath, I just did not know what to do next. After I picked up my race fuel belt consisting of all the necessary nutrition and first aid kit, I made a quick pee in the loo. It had been a long 9 hours since I last went to the loo!

Oh my god! I could barely squat. I had to do a quick one bending my knees slightly while standing and off I went.

Starting the run, the mercury started to rise, along with the humidity it was going to be a battle of the strongest and the weakest runners. I could see the difference in how some of the best Asians handling the heat better than some of the New Zealanders and Australians. I was pacing myself efficiently.

The run course was beautiful with two loops around lake and tracts consisting of a mixture of roads, wooden planks and sealed gravel. The gravel around the lake in our initial few kilometres was "therapeutic" as they were pointing against the soles of my feet. I was sure it could actually help me when I run later. In reality, it felt torturous. Wondering how I might alleviate the feeling of running along the painful path, I remembered how my friends and I had been running the trails of MacRitchie Reservoir way back in Singapore.

It took me about few kilometres of walk before my legs felt good heading out onto a run. The discomfort also slowly decreased the moment the path turned smooth. My body was just going through the motion, while I focused on getting my body to stay as sharp as possible in getting my nutrition and hydration down in to my body system regularly. Due to the increased heat and humidity, I was taking my salts more frequently. Proper hydration was key. I had a quick look at my watch and I was counting the pace I was going and how much time

I had left. I quickly found my rhythm which saw me gaining a smaller gap towards the faster cyclists. I was definitely not a 3- or 4-hour marathoner, so I would be glad if I could complete the marathon in less than 7 hours.

There was a stretch of parklands aside the old railway track. The way the bolts put these wooden planks together made it unbelievably challenging for anyone who were running after 3.8 kilometres of swim and 180 kilometres on the bike. I had been running for years – but I had not been trained to run on wooden planks. They were absorbing every ounce of energy I had while I was careful not to run onto the bolts. I had been on the stretch for about an hour, and ahead was about at least another 10-kilometre stretch. Aside from water and isotonic drink, the aid stations offered bananas, gel, salts and energy bars.

I was running on the wooden planks next to an old railway track.

Chris had strategically positioned himself so that he could keep my energy up.

"How're you doing?" Chris quietly whispered.

"I'm doing alright. This is the Ironman, Chris." I laughed

He laughed as if this was just another training session and he continued to cheer me.

As we made for our second loop on the run course, the crowds near the finishing line were starting to hinder in my run. The heat could be felt. Up to that point, I was cruising along at 8 minutes per kilometre pace. I knew it would get me off the course with sufficient time.

Then darkness fell. I felt lonely on the run, as there were not many supporters around. Volunteers at aid station also became less. Sponges, cokes, bananas, hydration were not refilled. There was not a photographer along the entire road. Suddenly this was not the Ironman race you had in mind or you had watched on the youtube all these while. It was only myself, and my soul along this stretch of lonesome endless road.

A cool breeze brushed past me as I jogged past the city. I just had a few more kilometres in front of me before I reached my special aids station. The sport had now reduced to a simple game.

Sof, you just need to follow the running path and enjoy, commit to it and do the best of your ability til you see the finish line. Just keep going.

As I slowly jogged, I looked around me – the sounds of the cricket, the flashing lights of the neon lights on the roofs of houses, the words on the tri top of the athlete in front of me, anything to keep my mind busy to watch out for.

The aid station near the 28-kilometre mark near their homes was innovative, as they prepared real food as part of athletes support. They prepared home cooked food like green bean soup, noodles and red tea. These went easy on our stomach.

Suddenly I found my gap kept narrowing, and soon I found myself in the same second loop with several men. In the final 18 kilometres, I felt relaxed as I made a change of socks. Perhaps I was a little too relaxed, as I found myself bitten with all the mosquitoes near the special needs aid station. As I passed my can of potato chips and snacks from my special needs bag to a nearby student volunteer, I continued my run for the rest of the leg. I took what I had, and I did what I could to keep myself moving.

On my last few kilometres, Richard approached me and asked if I was alright. I knew he had not proceeded to the run leg. I felt a sense of disappointment. But I was determined, and I gained more willpower to finish.

"I will be waiting for you near the finish line", he continued riding back to the finish line.

No matter the cost, I was going to make it. I nodded. The story kept repeating inside me as I continued running.

As I passed the wooden planks on my last loop, one jogger saw me and said, "You are still running! When are you going to stop?"

"Finishing. Finishing. And good bye!" I smiled at him. I continued running at a good pace of 8 minutes per kilometre.

The darkness of my battle broke when, with less than two kilometres to go, the distant glow of the finish line lights came into view. Then, with less than four hundred metres to go, Richard came towards me near the finish line. He joined me as we ran towards the finish line together. If this was an Ironman-brand event, I would have been disqualified. I just did not care as we had come so far for so long. Richard was going nuts, waving his arms and screaming as if he was the one finishing the race, smiling and shouting, "Yes! Yes!"

I finished the race in less than sixteen hours, one hour faster than what I had expected. For that moment, it felt so unreal. I knew I was aiming to make it in less than seventeen hours. But for me to break the sixteen hours, it was just unbelievable.

Well done, girl! You broke the sixteenth hour. This is much better than what you had imagined! A message sent my Australian friend Jamie came through my handphone.

Somehow, I did not cry. In fact, I was happy. This was it; this was what a full iron-distance triathlon was all about.

As I sat down on a chair, finishers were served with drinks and snacks.

I was wondering, "Would this be considered as finishing an Ironman? Did brand really matter?" As of now, the brand didn't seem to matter.

The story was simple: I was this girl who could not swim or cycle, and I was living my life in someone's expectations for every part of my life, right to even the choice of a life partner. I did not grow up thinking I want to be a world champion. Even when I started triathlon, I just wanted to see what and how far I could go. Never in my years on earth have I ever thought I would finish a full iron-distance triathlon sport.

I carried the belief that I have "it" in me in order to achieve "it". Without this belief, it just won't happen. My limits did not stop at where my parents thought I was. I guessed this was just that most people won't, and are contented with letting it be a fantasy or a dream, or perhaps on the "maybe someday" list. People focus on all the reasons why they won't instead of all the reasons why they can.

I blamed no one, as it seemed no point of doing so. I gained something in life, and I lost some or perhaps too much in life too. I too could stand on the sidelines of the finisher's chute watching but never acting.

But to actually being in the finisher's chute?

No words could ever describe it until I find it out for myself.

Now I looked back and thought to myself, "What if I had not taken the chance?"

Chapter 16

All or Nothing

Many stories stopped at just completing a big race. Once I officially became an Ironman, I asked myself what this Ironman meant to me. Years ago, I was a determined and petite girl who seemed to have something to prove. The sport then played an immensurable role in making the change in me, setting the path for me to move towards enjoying and appreciating the process of training, learning more about myself, and coping with all these adversities. Even if it is just one person of whom I can inspire and chase his or her dreams, I will gladly do so.

In the race, every minute counts. The sport made me seek out every opportunity out there and make every single minute of my life count.

The full iron-distance triathlon for Challenge Taiwan was cancelled a year later. Had I not taken the opportunity, the realisation of my dream would perhaps take a longer time.

Or never.

⎯⎯◈⎯⎯

The next day, aside from sitting on the bed with shattered legs, trying to scrub off those sticky numbers from my arms, peeling off the sunburnt skin, and going to the toilet more often than usual due to a cranky digestive system, I also suffered numbness and a lack of strength on my fingers and palms. I could hardly grab a can of coke, open the door, or even hold a pair of chopsticks. It could be a result of some compression on the nerves of my palms due to the tight grip on my handlebars. I guessed all these did not matter. I have finished the full iron-distance triathlon.

As I was packing my luggage, separating the filthy sweaty gears from all the dryer ones, I had a good look at my Challenge Taiwan finisher t-shirt. No matter how many of these races I attempt, I know that I will only ever get this special one.

Then, I took a step back and reconnected with everything else in the world that was still existing and just as important in my life. Although Richard was happy with my finish, I was emotionally connected with Richard who did not finish his race. Chris's birthday was coming; I had not planned for my weekly date with my mum; my bills were due for payment at the end of the week; and I even remembered I had a huge meeting in office the next two days.

I had been walking up and down the streets of Taiwan, and I had been buying non-stop all the forbidden foods prior to a race. I was looking for comfort street food like ice-cream, iced milk tea, deep fried chicken cutlets, and oyster omelet. Chris was looking at me as if I looked like a scavenger, and as if I had not been eating for days. This was just part of after-race experience.

I supposed this was also the recovery, the chance to cycle around the streets for a while, to take stock and to put everything in perspective. This was also a chance for me to look ahead in the future, and asked myself exactly what I want from this sport and in my life. In my late thirties, I still had so much to aim for. Yet it seemed there were so many signs that my body clock was warning against me.

The first thing I noticed upon getting off the plane when I returned to Singapore was that the triathlon sport was steadily building up with all the bike bags and triathletes from different countries. The triathlon journey also provided the full range of excellence in terms of world records, thrills, spills, drama, and occasional disappointment to keep athletes back on the training field, and to keep moving forward in life. Somehow, there was still a big part of me that I wanted to keep on developing and improving myself.

The priority now seemed to be focusing on this family planning target --- The Medal Project. Singapore was celebrating her 50th year. A special medal was given to every child born in the year 2015.

Family planning has been frustrating. It was incredibly draining looking back the path we had taken, and I just have to deal with it.

I went through a three-month period of which I had no control of – scheduled visits to my gynaecologist, going through a series of tests and taking supplements and medication. The early weeks of this period were a piece of cake. I could still do as much exercise as I could with my swimming, cycling, and running up to 50 kilometres a week. During the stimulation of my ovaries phase, I had Richard helping me with the injections of up to about fifty or more. His hands shivered, and his perspiration rolled down his forehead for every jab he gave me.

When my ovaries swelled to huge sizes, I was still doing long rides. Perhaps I was just riding to take my mind off this Medal Project. My gynaecologist also got used to my fitness regime, and wondered how I could do such intense activity under such short supply of blood in my body. The thought of not exercising for so long during an incredibly stressful time was unfathomable!

I just could not take it just doing nothing. On top of these, I felt like a sick lady receiving huge dosages of progesterone which caused fatigue in my body every few hours. The development process was just too long for me to bear. The most stressful part of knowing if I was pregnant was however a quick one. We received news that our Medal Project had failed.

Undoubtedly, we were tired in all aspects whether financially, physically or mentally. Yet Richard and I did not take it negatively. We just moved on.

It was three days to Langkawi Ironman. For a short moment, Richard and I were torn as to whether we should go for the race. We had already got ready all our registration, hotel, and air tickets and had even applied leave from our work.

My gynaecologist gave the green light for me to ride. I did not tell him there would be a marathon after the bike leg. It just did not matter any way. Taking some time off to enjoy our break in Langkawi after all these stresses was key. Whether we could finish the race was secondary.

As the day of the Langkawi Ironman race approached, my anxiety level rose. I spent nights lying awake, trying to figure out what to do. At times I would think: *Screw it. I kept lying to myself that I could do this --- The Langkawi Ironman.*

Just before the race, a river of images and memories flooded my mind. Meeting the seasoned veteran athletes, their detached look, their branded speed suit and goggles, I took a deep breath and started as best as I could.

It was a no wetsuit swim in the comfortable warm waters of Langkawi beaches. Amidst the flat with a little chop in the murky waters, it was a rolling start for the athletes. Lane ropes also guided each batch of athletes as they entered the water to start the race.

What really killed many athletes was the hilly bike course. They were typical Malaysia roads, just like that of Tour de Langkawi. While the trees protected athletes from the sun, the roads were not smooth, and possessed lots of little rocks along the way. We had every opportunity to pass through local villages, nature parks and plenty of hills.

Cycling past several undulating hills at the initial 15 kilometres, I checked my speedometer. My speed remained pretty consistent at about 25 kilometres per hour. After my warm-up, my heart rate slowly crept upwards, up to about 85 percent maximum heart beat rate. This was not a good sign at the beginning of a big race like this.

After 30 kilometres, I started to feel the lethargy, followed by a sharp rise in my core body temperature. I had experienced heat in many races, but somehow I was not able to keep cool for this one. At that point, I was still feeling no power at all.

At about 50 kilometres, many athletes struggled against fatigue on the "Red Bull Tough Zone" which was about 10 kilometres long with roads going skywards with some five-kilometre sharp and steep climbs, steep descents and sweeping bends, and through a cave tunnel. The roads in the bike course were not closed, so everyone had to take caution of the drivers around the island.

What was also a sight was that along the bike course, the children stood right on the edge of the roads with their hands out for a high-five as athletes rode past. Hydration at aid stations was sufficient, but many athletes stopped, crowded around the aid stations, and dumped themselves down with lots of hydration whenever available.

After cycling for just about 60 kilometres, I did not feel good. I was having hot flushes and profuse sweating. I was dumping more salt tablets into my body more regularly than usual. At about 70 kilometres into the bike leg, I was having heart palpitations with my heart thumping for a few seconds from time to time. Due to the fatigue and my weak health conditions, I was cautious not to push myself to the extent of damaging my body system. I was putting in more than 95 percent maximum heart beat rate effort throughout, and did not feel good with the over dosage of salt and all other medication in me.

After I came out of the "Red Bull Tough Zone", I took a quick look at my watch, and told myself that I needed a sign from God if I should continue my second loop.

At 75-kilometre mark, God sent me a tyre puncture. The bike mechanic came to help me, and I actually asked him to take his time. I had discussed with Richard before the race started. If I did not finish my first loop within 4 hours 15 minutes, I would not go on. It was 4 hours 19 minutes on my watch. I ended my journey here, and decided not to proceed upon reaching the 90-kilometre mark. I knew there was no going back.

The marshal asked why I did not proceed in the race, and I just gave a shake on my head. Thinking of it now, how I wish the marshal had asked me one more time or pushed me to keep going. It is a true regret for missing an opportunity to have simply been a good triathlete and stopping only when prompted to by a marshal.

The race volunteer took off my timing chip, and that was it: I was out of the race. It might have been just as devastating to many athletes who probably got their timing chips removed too. It did not change the fact that my efforts also fell short. Somehow my mind went blank.

With all those years of training, racing, and believing in myself, I was still at least a few minutes short of what I could do on my first loop. I unclipped myself from the bike, and chatted with some of the people we knew who were supporting the race. Some of my friends were stunned. My huge expectations on myself just could not match with what my body was physically accepting.

It sounded strange, but I never tell anyone like that, all of it. Telling the truth did not feel good for me. In fact, it hurt; my heart was racing as I recalled my ride like I was on the big climb throughout the entire race. But even in that pain, giving up seemed like a big step forward, and that it was the right thing to do at that point in time. I could probably be harboring all the excuses, but the reality was: my heart was just not committed to this race.

Was I just not the Ironman I thought I was?

I returned to the hotel, made my change before I went back to the course to support the other athletes who were still racing. Humidity remained high, and hydration remained crucial. Near the finish line of the bike leg, I saw the sweeper truck sending athletes back to the transition point. These were the ones who could not make it to the bike cut-off. I too found it hard to accept when I saw two male athletes who just missed the bike cut-off by less than five seconds. And these were athletes who finished the entire 3.8-kilometre swim and 180-kilometre bike route.

As I continued to cheer for my friends who completed the bike leg, I turned to Richard and asked to return to the hotel. It was just difficult for me to keep watching the athletes racing but yet it was one race, which I would not wallow in sorrows.

I then returned to Singapore, and soon the disappointment of not completing Ironman Langkawi was forgotten. A few days went by, and I was thinking if I should be going for my Ironman Western Australia, which I had signed up earlier in the year.

When someone decided to sign up for such an event like an iron-distance triathlon, it was not a decision made lightly. For me, Langkawi and Western Australia were supposed to be my backup plans. Ironman Western Australia was in first week of December. These races were not the kind you would start training only for the month before the race. You needed to buy expensive bike equipment, shoes, nutrition, specific clothing items and train for the race. My working schedule and lifestyle needed to change and time spent with my dear ones need to be planned and rescheduled. More importantly, taking good care of my health was needful. Earlier this year for Challenge Taiwan, I was making good progress and achieved my target. Now down with the failure of the Medal Project, I lost a couple of months of training, and definitely my mental mind for completing a full iron-distance triathlon.

What was I going for in this race? I had not purchased any accommodation. Neither had I purchased any air flight tickets for the trip to Perth. It all seemed very clear, and was an easy decision to make. Yet, I found it was a hard choice for me to give up Western Australia Ironman 2014. With all these family planning frustrations going on, I knew my heart was no longer on a full iron-distance triathlon.

The lesson in Langkawi also made my choice easier: I withdrew from the Western Australia Ironman race.

Regardless of whether we are achieving our targets we have in mind be it a triathlon, having a child, changing a person, or climbing the corporate ladder, the process of trying often takes a toll on us. While we can blame on everything else or everyone else, often it is us ourselves who can deal with these moments.

⟡

Chapter 17

Live with No Regrets

It was a month after the Langkawi Ironman has ended. I felt miserable, just like how Graeme Obree felt when his individual pursuit for world champion saw him took and lost the world one-hour distance record.

It was not about my attempt on any redemption. After I had completed races of such scale, it had gone beyond proving to anyone that I could finish another full iron-distance triathlon. Richard and I became serious in the sport because we wanted to. We no longer treated triathlon just like another weekend event. Richard did not just tag along for a ride. In fact, he grew interested in my racing equipment and enjoyed seeing me racing.

Every breakfast, I would sit upright with my cup of latte, and start scribbling on pieces of papers. Richard has always been open to new ideas, and everything I learnt about training, nutrition, performance and the sport. Richard listened intensively as if I had all the answers to all the problems, and I always wished I had. It was amazing how we would look up for resources like the web or the library to tackle the different challenges. After dinner, Richard and I spent our time discussing about our race schedule, our training, our equipment and our performance.

One day over dinner, I asked him, "What strategy did you use for Challenge Taiwan Ironman?"

"Race conservatively, swim within the cut-off, go all out on the bike, and run or walk with whatever I have left on the run." This was his reply.

"Wouldn't you be doing what Chris Lieto has been doing, pushing on his bike and desire to win but always fail to have the fastest running split in the field?" I questioned him further.

In Kona Ironman 2011, Craig Alexander and Chrissie Wellington ran the fastest marathons. Miranda Carfrae's run and win in Kona Ironman World Championship 2014 emphasised the importance of a strong run in a triathlon. These professionals all played to their strengths and outran their competitors.

Techniques, numbers, names and stories – these were so often shared between Richard and I. I never liked physics in school but we started to talk about chain ring size, rear cog size, friction brakes, wheel size and power as if we could teach a course on speed.

Instead of our usual routine day to day training rides, we recognise that years of hard work are still crucial in developing a base big enough to be able to race at a higher intensity over long distance triathlons. Our training rides in Singapore, and several countries like Bintan had definitely proven their worth. Of course, there are many "physical beasts" who will log in huge endurance mileage a few months before a big race.

In the world of triathlon, there were many stories of strong athletes who focused on building their strength to build up their form. Chris McCormack, winner of 2007 Ironman World Championship, did not lose his strength while losing his weight for the race. Recognising the need for strengthening with a good mix of racing strategy, Richard and I planned our training and race schedule for the year ahead.

The way I raced when I signed up the running races in the past reminded me: I did not want to put myself into situations that drag me back into the black hole such that I realised I had paid hundreds and even thousands of dollars on registration fees at the end of the year.

Richard and I even made a pact that if we take home the million dollar or sometimes six million dollar winnings from our lottery purchase, we will travel to a couple of countries on our bucket list we raced in – Cebu, Vietnam, Bintan, wherever – and do something different to improve the race experience. It could be leading a volunteering programme in producing bikes for the low-income children or educating the underprivileged women in supporting races. In fact, I would think of every way I could to make a positive difference to the world. But in reality, I had to admit one or six million dollars is a lot of money for the underdeveloped countries. What can I not do with that sum of money?

After two years of riding on all kinds of terrains in Singapore, and in neighbouring countries, I recognised that Tour de Bintan was the closest thing I could come to as an Union Cycliste Internationale (UCI) organised and sanctioned event. The UCI is the world's governing body in the sport of bicycle racing, so it was a big thing to me to participate in such a race. The notion of racing and completing Tour de Bintan voiced down to the need for me to gear up in terms of fitness, strength and endurance.

The Tour de Bintan course indeed promised big hilltop climbs, sweltering heat of up to 38 degree Celsius, dust, mud, and headwinds. The race began with a prologue criterium on Friday, determining who would ride which category for the next two days. With our bikes well-handled and safely stored by the event organiser, we were very much relieved of handling this major part of logistics.

The Gran Fondo was a 150-kilometre journey through the north and east of Bintan over mostly rolling roads. While most women would have joined the 135-kilometre Women category, I joined Richard in the Gran Fondo category. While the pace remained brutal for those who were in the Cat 1 race category, Cat 2 race category cyclists consisted of several Cat 1 cyclists from previous years making the race a war of attrition.

Unlike the cycling leg in triathlons, there were cycling rules to abide by --- no aero or tribars, no back bottle cages, no aero-helmets, no sleeveless cycling tops, and no compression wear. All of which I had to admit, it was quite tough for me especially when I had only one bottle cage on my bike.

At the carnival-like atmosphere at the starting point, I saw the leader of the M Riders.

"Hi, Sean. Remember us?" We called him. He was the same guy who laughed at us when we showed our interest in the race a year ago.

"Oh hi!" he replied.

He did not say anything else. I just smiled at him. I just wanted to show him I too could stand at the start line just like him.

We saw cyclists of all sizes, the tall ones and the obese ones. The atmosphere made me feel as though I was a pro cyclist going for Tour de France. The front peloton rode like shooting stars while Richard and I soon found ourselves at the very back with less than twenty cyclists in sight.

Using a couple as our rabbit, Richard and I watched our distance markers and speed on our speedometers as we rode comfortably at average 22 to 24 kilometres per hour up to 50 kilometres. With several clayey hills of up to 15 percent gradient, we definitely felt like Kings of the Mountain as we conquered them. The descent was not narrow but was winding, with a steep drop at corners at times. Halfway through, we could feel other cyclists dreading the day. They dreaded the pain and you could feel their pain as many held their quads as they rode. For those cyclists who started out harder than their sustainable workload, they began to drop below that workload due to accumulated fatigue from their earlier efforts. Making it to the next cut-off became more challenging as the route ahead was filled with more hills.

Recalling my weekend tempo training rides, I prayed hard as the pace ahead definitely required some concentration. Not remembering the exact distance for the next cut-off point, I remained focused, and kept pedaling. At one of the climbs, I saw this guy who murmured, and hung his head down on his saddle.

I shouted, "You can do it."

He said, "I can't."

This did not mean it was easy for me. The long day definitely wore on our legs. Many cycling club members dropped away one by one. Some rode strongly up the hills but cramped up and fell off their bikes. Richard too suffered before the 126-kilometre cut-off. We suffered even more as the second last aid station ran out of water. That kind of depletion could make strange things happen. I had two choices – to give up now since there was no more water, or perhaps I could still continue and perhaps I could still finish. There was this guy who applauded me as he saw I did not stop to rest. I told him I was not done yet, as I still had another 50 kilometres to go. I kept going. I was still keeping time. An hour was left and soon I had about 30 kilometres in front of me.

One of the cyclists talked to me and said, "I don't think we can make it to cut-off time".

"Don't care about cut-off time!" I shouted.

I felt a level of adrenaline that I had never felt before. His words did put me under some kind of panic or pressure you may called it. At this point, I badly wanted to finish this race, as I had come so far. The action was intense with me chasing towards the finish line. I had nothing left in my bento bag, no salt tablet, no gel, no food. Every revolution of the pedals sapped me more, and it was a question of sufficiency of fuel and calories in my body.

The concept of having enough soon came to light. I told myself I had enough in me, to just relax and ride my pace, and not to push it. Without doubt, I saw some cyclists who were cheating, as they held their hands onto passing motorbikes. That gave me a lot of encouragement to persevere to finish.

With four hundred metres to the finish line, I could hear the announcements playing in the background. As I crossed the finish line and I heard my name being called, I felt a sense of grandeur and elation. At the end of the day, as Richard and I climbed up onto the bus picking us back to the hotel, I saw how everyone was physically shattered.

My world exploded in happy pandemonium. That day, I kept staring at my medal. It felt so good as if I had won the Tour De Bintan. I gained a full understanding of why the Tour could be the hardest event in the world. This was just different from the Langkawi climb experience. In race cycling, race tactics determine race outcomes far more than just physical ability alone. Some cyclists were stunned by the severity of the climb, and some simply could not keep up with the front of the pack. While I overheard a group of finishers mentioning about certain cycling tactics such as attack as a form of swift acceleration, breakaway to create a gap between cyclists, and bridge to close the distance between cyclists, bike racing sure required creativity to come into play and to look for new ways to improve performance. While I earned a whole new experience in terms of bike racing, it reminded me to keep moving forward. During my recovery period, I realised I should not be reflexively filling in the empty voids with just another race or another trip to somewhere.

Life will never be the same with the loss of our dear ones, leaving a mark in our hearts which can never be removed or replaced. I do not do half or full iron-distance triathlon just to let people know that I could do it. Neither do I participate in such hardcore races for some fund-raising causes or to save lives. I commit to such races more of in the hope of sparing another person the pain by sharing what I had experienced through.

<hr />

The year 2014 ended as a gentle reminder to get myself back to shape. When FINA and Singapore Swimming Association brought in some of the best World Swimmers, I was one of the lucky few who got selected to meet Jessica Hardy, an American International swimmer who won 28 medals in Olympics, World and Pan Pacific and Fabio Scozzoli, an Italian gold medalist in World Swimming Championship. These professional swimmers do their swims every morning, wherever they are in the world. While these athletes' events are often short and explosive, they do a lot more cross-training like plyometric and strengthening exercises outside the water. They too advised against training too hard and getting injured in the process of reaching our goals.

I was whipping up a dish with Swimmer Gold Medalist Fabio Scozzoli.

Being disciplined and following our training schedule was just as tough as sticking to my dietary plans in the past. Many races out there still tempt us. Our strategy and training plans went off-course a little. It wasn't perfect strategically speaking. Before Christmas in 2014, I was given an opportunity to run the Standard Chartered Marathon Singapore. Not many people were selected and given this opportunity. And it was definitely too tempting to say no.

With less than two times a week of running, I was not expecting too much in terms of running a good time, and so I finished the marathon with a run and walk strategy. I was having a slow time but I had a great enjoyable race as I suffered less fatigue and muscle pain.

I was glad I still have it in me. To say it was an ugly display of lack of fitness and endurance was an understatement. This race was a test of core fitness and patience-testing, especially when I had to instill the discipline of walking at a certain pace.

⊰⊱

After all the Christmas and New Year feasting, my fitness was to be further tested in the new year. Our aspirations ran high and Richard decided it was time for us to step up and give ourselves a different kind of challenge. He is always on the lookout for challenges, and it rubs off on me to ignite that spark of light in me. There is nothing like starting that fire within me to help me to know myself better.

This was like the Olympic Games to me. The journey to my own Games had just started with a new race plan charted in our exercise log book.

Before Labour Day holiday, which is a holiday in Singapore, Richard asked me if I could complete Busselton Ironman 70.3 in Australia. The cut-off time was 7.5 hours, and not 8.5 hours. This alone sounded tough to me facing the well-known Busselton winds. Richard further increased the stake and challenged me if I could join him and complete another half iron-distance triathlon the week after Busselton.

I replied, "Why not?"

This was not another half marathon and back to back with a full marathon like the Disney races we had gone through. We were talking about back to back half iron-distance triathlon races, and they were all new races to me. While Busselton held its 70.3 races in a relatively cool climate, Da Nang on the other hand was an inaugural 70.3 race held in extremely hot tropical climate.

You sure you want to do this?

Was I 100 percent ready for this crazy challenge? My mind kept wondering.

I was still recovering from vertigo. For several months, I had been feeling giddy whenever I lay down in bed or turned my head. At first, I thought it was my usual low blood pressure. I just could not swim, do any yoga, or even sleep well as the world felt like it was constantly spinning around me. Then I realised it never really go away until I was referred to the hospital for a checkup and underwent a series of physiotherapy sessions. Such luck I had when I thought I just recovered from my eye condition, and now I was suffering another condition. It took me several months to get over this vertigo condition.

Meanwhile, I was checking online for air ticket prices, schedule, accommodation prices, car rentals, and aligning with the range of race activities. I could not believe I had just signed up for the wrong race. I had just signed up for the full Busselton Ironman race. It was a huge mistake. After much pleading with the Race Organiser and holding some faith in the wonders of the Triathlon sport, I received a confirmation to the Busselton Ironman 70.3 race two weeks before race day. By then, most accommodation near the race site were almost filled. I felt lucky as the Gods helped me to find an only room left near the race site at the very last minute. Everything seemed to be falling into place perfectly.

Three weeks before race day, Richard fell sick. He had been coughing non-stop and had fever for almost the entire week. The week after, it was my turn. I was feeling cold and had a fever too. After much rest and seeing the doctor, my body temperature was still not going down. Being afraid that I had dengue, I consulted another doctor.

"I have a race next week. Can I have a jab so that I can have my body temperature lowered?" I visited the doctor, and made a sincere request.

"No....you shouldn't go for any triathlons. You have to rest." The doctor was adamant on this. My persistence on going for the race definitely stunned the doctor as it was all shown on her face.

Ya right. How much do you know about registering for an overseas race and not able to go for it? Do you know the amount of hard work that went into the preparation for this race?

My mind started to complain.

"You athletes just don't understand. You read newspapers, don't you? Do you know why there are so many athletes who died in races?" The doctor asked.

As I switched off my ears, she rattled off names and stories of accidents and deaths. As I rolled my eyes, Richard was smiling at me in the corner.

"I will give you a stronger dosage of antibiotics. I think I better key in the information that you came to look for me. I am your last doctor before your race. Just in case." The doctor looked worried.

Richard and I laughed. All I wanted was a jab to lower my body temperature!

Fortunately, towards the end of the week, my body temperature dropped. However, I was still not feeling optimal.

Two days before the race day, I tried swimming in the cold waters of Busselton. I rode against the winds, of which I had not experienced before in Singapore. They were probably about 20 kilometres per hour or more. There was no time for worry. The race was two days away and I could only prepare myself that much for a race. I just prayed that the weather would be a better one the next day.

Busselton Ironman 70.3 fell on a Saturday. Just like at any other races, athletes crowded around the swim start to see the professionals being flagged off. As the ladies stood at the back awaiting for their wave to start, one Australian lady turned around and asked me, "Are you nervous?"

"Take it easy", I said.

"Look at me, I am an Asian. You have bigger lungs. You will swim faster than me. One stroke at a time, you will reach there." I assured her.

I could not believe myself what I had just said. Swimming had always been my weakest leg, and here I was advising another athlete in a race.

I tried out the waters in Busselton Australia a day before race day.

The race started with a 15 degree Celsius wet suit swim around the beautiful jetty. The extreme cold weather was a challenge to me as I could feel my ears going numb in the waters. I had prepared myself mentally but I could only do that much in assimilating the weather a few days before race day. The waters looked deceivingly calm. It was a long swim out, followed by a short turn before turning back to the shore. Unlike those races in Singapore, there was no line guiding athletes in the swim throughout the entire swim course.

As I swam about 100 metres out, I could see the bottom of the sea with the sea weeds underneath the waters. With most of the athletes already way ahead of me, they were pulling further and further away from me. Then, the next wave of athletes came along fast and furious. I could not catch their drafts at all. They were either too fast or I was just too slow. Scenes of Geelong flashed in my mind.

Oh God please, not again.

Come on, you can do this. You just need to reach the first buoy. After that, it will be easier as the underwater currents will change.

While I thought I was not moving much at about 400 metres away from shore, I changed my swimming technique and pushed myself forward with some consistency in my strokes. At the sight of the first brightly coloured buoy, it felt like I had found gold in the sea. With the persistent underwater currents, I felt a little imbalanced as I thought I lost my navigation after the second turn. I had no time to worry if it was my vertigo or it was just me. I just followed the silver cappers right in front of me and kept swimming. With an easier return swim, I finally finished the 1.9-kilometre swim.

"Yes!" I shouted.

The sun was out by then. I removed my wetsuit, prepared myself for the bike course and off I went. With two big loops of 45 kilometres, the challenge of the bike course was not about the terrain as it was largely flat. Richard who was supporting me at the side cheered me on as I tried to smile and continued with my second loop.

Going at about 28 kilometres per hour for my first lap, I suddenly faced the head winds near the beach on my second lap. With a petite size like me, I faced great difficulty having to control my bike as the winds hit me. I tried to go at a higher cadence in a lower gear as my legs just could not hold the power towards the long forested stretch against the strong winds. I just continued and aimed to reach the end of the road at a consistent speed of 25 kilometres per hour.

The roads were long and lonely. It was all mental just like when I was training all alone back in Singapore. I did not turn back in the fear of being the only one left behind. I believed if I kept holding on, I would reach the u-turn point. It was cross-winds after the u-turn, those you could feel on your wheels. I just kept going. I saw several athletes pushing their bikes as I cruised along. At about 5 kilometres near the finish line, this guy came along with a loud screeching sound. His wheels caught fire and this might be a flat. I went consistently at about 26 kilometres per hour, leaving some legs for running.

When I reached the transition, I made a quick change of gears, took a quick bite on my sandwich, sip my Gatorade energy drink and I was ready to run my three laps. I looked down at my pants, and saw salt all over my pants. I diligently followed up what I needed to do, and took in my nutrition. I caught my breath, lowered my heart beat rate and kept moving my legs. To finish two laps, it was already mental. My strategy was no strategy. *Just keep going and no walking.* I said to myself. In my final lap, my quads started to hurt. Every pounding on the ground pulled every tendons and muscles in my knees right up to my quads.

To finish my last lap in my run, I had one strategy: with every 100 to 200 running counts, I walked 30 steps. As I walked, I saw this tall guy and motivated him to keep going near the finish line. Shortly after he crossed the finish line, I sprinted my final 50 metres with my arms raised. It felt just like the first time I finished my 70.3. I cried. It was my Geelong experience that gave me this achievement of 6 hours 55 minutes – a time I couldn't ask for a better one. Richard's face was beaming with joy, just like an angelic face, that kept me going. He always believes in me. I had to put some faith in myself, and not wallow on my past lessons.

After my success in Busselton, the biggest physical challenge was how to dial things down before going for the next race the week after. Way back in Singapore, I had heard stories of friends who were doing two, three or even four races in a season. A frequent racer's success also did not last as I saw them hurt, burnt up within one to two years of doing this triathlon sport, or trying to get a slot to Kona (which was believed to be the great daddy of the full iron-distance triathlon) and then leaving the sport.

The next half iron-distance triathlon was happening this following week. *Everything was set. There was no turning back for me.*

Although I had finished a couple of half iron-distance triathlon races, I did not underestimate Da Nang Ironman 70.3 in Vietnam. My participation in Da Nang Ironman 70.3 was important with valuable insights from racing in a Third World country like Vietnam. The excitement of racing in an inaugural race like 70.3 in Vietnam kept me motivated. While some friends were hesitating over joining a new race, I felt I just had to be part of this fun. This is what life is all about - trying out new things everyday!

Just because I was feeling pumped up for the race, this did not mean I had it easy on my recovery of a strained muscle on my right hamstring and calves from Bussleton race. Each of us has 24 hours each day. With six days to go minus race day, this left me with 144 hours. I did not spend on things that just kept me busy like sitting on the bed doing nothing. I was consistently using my massage ball to reduce muscle tension and to improve flexibility on my right knee.

I only had so many days of great form, and I did not want to waste them. With the ache, I did not go for the bike reccee. I did not go for the run trial. To address anxiety and boost confidence, I visualised the entire race in my head again and again. I planned to go in easy on the flat bike course with 75 percent maximum heart beat rate, and probably up to 85 percent on a climb up a single bridge. I did not go for any bike reccee as I needed the much rest. I clenched my fist telling myself I was in control of the race. I want to finish this challenge. And I will.

The non-wet suit swim started in the clear waters of Da Nang with no fish in sight. We were lucky that the waters in the morning at the beach front on China Beach proved to be less turbulent than those in the afternoon. With the shallow waters at the start, it helped shorter athletes like me to run further out before diving in. That morning, I finished the swim in less than an hour though the waters were a little choppy. With the pristine white beaches, clean waters and palm trees, the host country, Da Nang was gracious with their people enjoying and watching the athletes racing through their environment under the basking hot sun.

The bike course provided great views of both new and modern Da Nang with high rises and fisherman villages. The flat smooth bike course allowed the faster cyclists to go all out. The closed bike course did not necessarily mean that the roads were empty as several Vietnamese motorbikes cruised through some of the smaller lanes.

Strong winds however added some trepidation to the race, causing some headwinds on the bike course and tight u-turns.

While I cruised along the bike course, I saluted and admired the Vietnamese athletes going strong on their bikes especially when triathlon was still very new in Third World Countries. At about 40th kilometre, I saw Richard on the bike course on his few return laps. He could still smile, so obviously he was enjoying this heat more than I was!

As the winds cooled off the perspiration from the athletes, many athletes could not feel the heat coming. Several athletes started having trouble staying down on their aero-bars. At the last lap, and under the immense heat, the last aid station, which was about 15 kilometres away from the bike finish, proved to be crucial in a race like half iron-distance triathlon. Athletes took in their hydration, and drenched their heads with water as they rode on.

In my last 10 kilometres on my bike, I was blessed with a passing Vietnamese supporter cheering for me on his motorbike. Although we had differences in our language, the Vietnamese's support motivated and kept me going. This was what made it common between the two of us. Pushing my bike under the heat to the second transition was easy. Coming out of the transition was tough. For that short few minutes, I was confused in identifying exactly what I wanted or expected of the race and of my body under that kind of heat. I had made my change of gear, grabbed my isotonic drink, and finished a packet of gel and salt tablet. They did not kick in immediately as my heart rate went skyrocketing high.

Despite the run course was a flat 10 kilometres out and u-turn back, the run was simply grueling. I had never felt so hot until I could feel the sun burning through my skin every minute. It was 38 degree

Celsius but it felt like 43 degree Celsius. Every cup of ice I grabbed melted within 50 metres.

I looked pretty silly trying to run at a very slow probably about 9 minutes per kilometre pace walk. My heart beat rate was still going high at about 95 percent maximum heart beat rate under this heat. At about three kilometres on the run course, I tried to run and shuffle in the heat but I could not hold the pace at all. The slow run and jog strategy was not working, and I just could not understand this. My mind kept telling me I could do this, but I needed to figure out how. Quickly.

At the 5-kilometre mark, I grabbed some ice, chucked them inside my tri top, and placed them in front of my chest. I was also grabbing a bottle of cold water. Lowering my core temperature, I started to jog a little. The long 10-kilometre stretch proved endless as athletes kept moving forward. At the sight of the u-turn, I told myself to run throughout the rest of the run course. By then I caught up with Johnny, a Singapore triathlete friend. We chatted a little, encouraged each other and started to run together. It was a routine of running to the aid station, changing of cold water bottle, putting the ice next to my chest, and keeping a consistent pace in my run. As I started to feel the sun burning through my skin of my exposed arms, I poured the water from my bottle onto my body until I reached the next aid station. The heat and glare were staring right in front of me, so I started to half shut my eyes. That dark visualisation of an oasis in my mind helped me.

As I was approaching about two kilometres away from the finish line, I was still cheering for the athletes who were slowly walking in the opposing direction. Richard was one of them who by then, was about 7 kilometres behind me. He was still recovering from his cough and he was still walking. I could feel the lethargy hitting everyone's souls.

At the last five kilometres, I turned my head to see if Johnny was still with me. He was nowhere around. I must have kept myself too focused in my run, or I must have literally closed my eyes totally!

I slowed down to wait for Johnny. He still did not turn up, and I started to walk. I wanted to enjoy the last stretch of the race. With my adrenaline flowing, it was a moment of elation as what we had gone through was not just a half iron-distance triathlon race, but a test of our bodies under such heat. I finished the race in 7 hours 45 minutes, below the 8 hours 30 minutes cut-off, and I completed my back-to-back half iron-distance triathlons under these extreme weathers.

Three months after Da Nang Ironman 70.3, I sowed not only a string of continuous action in weekly swims, training rides and long runs, but I also reaped a certain character out of me.

1.9-kilometre swim, 90-kilometre bike, 21-kilometre run —- all these started to become so familiar to me.

By then, I have welcomed suffering as part of all of us going through such that I start to test myself. No matter what was going to happen, I learnt to embrace it, and to accept it, even though my body was telling me to quit.

Triathletes, by nature, are proud of our achievements. Some might be exaggerated – looking at a short rolling course and declaring it as hilly, sharing about morning til dawn workouts with intermittent breaks, and Kona-like hospitality refueling buffets. So undoubtedly, I heard about many good things about Cebu Ironman 70.3 races from many of my fellow friends who completed the race. This was one race I had put off for a long time. Well-known for its great hospitality, high quality event management, accompanied with its calm waters and flat course, Cebu Ironman 70.3 had indeed raised the expectations of many athletes.

Cebu Island, Philippines is about three-hour flight from Singapore. Although there were hiccups on sudden flight changes for our trip to Cebu, our arrival at Cebu Airport was thrilling with a sudden fire breakout from an annex building of the airport. For that moment, I thought my race was done for!

Our decision to stay in a cheaper alternative hotel two kilometres away from the race site proved insightful. We found that there is a lot of poverty, however these villagers are different from the impoverished.

In terms of their faith, families and friends, these villagers eat simple food like rice, bananas, sweet potatoes, small fishes and vegetables they grow themselves or farm from the sea.

Before the race had even started, we cycled our bikes out from our hotel to the race site, and we were very much welcomed by these villagers. The streets were decorated with Ironman, race and welcome banners from the airport all the way to the race site. Prior to the race, it was a sight of children running along the streets cheering for us "Ironman! Ironman!", and looking so happy and excited for us.

After we had passed through the villages, here we saw the white sand beaches and historical sites of Cebu which reflect its cosmopolitan past. Indeed, they offered majestic views of the mountains and seas.

Cebu, Philippines, known for its white sand beaches and historical sites that reflect its cosmopolitan past, indeed offered majestic views of the mountains and seas.

On the day before race day, we excitedly racked up our bike. The temperature was about 34 degree Celsius. After our usual familiarisation with our transition spot, swim exit, bike exit, and run exit, we were still wondering if signages would be set up on race day itself. The start list was a huge motivation to me with great champions like Craig Alexander and Luke McKenzie.

On race day, swimmers were waiting at a dedicated holding area according to their predicted swim times. The slower swimmers found a loop hole in the rolling start of the swim as they started off earlier.

I was still diligently following my wave in my predicted 50-minute completion time. As I swam out to the first, second and third buoy, it looked like a fast swim with schools of colourful fishes shimmering and darting in well-rehearsed unison below me. I felt relaxed with the sandy seafloor clearly visible beneath.

While taking some draft from the faster swimmers, I was attacked by the stronger water currents hitting around the long 850-metre stretch. I was not aware of how far I was from the next buoy. I kept swimming around the same area without having the buoy getting close to me at all. I pushed harder with a greater turnover of my arms in an attempt to push myself further. By then, groups of probably over fifty athletes were swimming around me, and many of them were stuck swimming around the same area. I somehow managed to swim away. However, anxiety grew as I knew I had little time left to cross that last buoy.

Amidst the chaotic situation, I overheard that the organiser had extended the swim to an extra ten minutes. The swim had taken a lot out of everyone. Richard completed the swim but was told that he did not make it to the swim cut-off and could not proceed in the race. Yet he saw several athletes were allowed to continue the race. Such unfairness!

Once I was out of the swim, my mind refocused on the bike leg. Here I experienced a fault on my race belt. I had placed my energy gels on my belt. Every time I pulled one out, the belt came off and I had to stop my bike to solve this problem. I also stopped to set up my speedometer which I had left it inside the bento box. As I lost a couple of minutes doing my so-called silly things, I reminded myself to check off every item on my checklist for my next race.

Roads in Cebu were flat with considerable climbs at bridges, tunnels and highways, but they were not smooth. Caution was taken not to ride hard over the roads to prevent tyre punctures. With headwinds coming from one stretch, it was tailwinds on the other. From holding onto the handlebars of Milou, I started to sit upright, and pedalled with higher cadence against the headwinds. I felt like Lance Armstrong, a strong cyclist known for his high cadence pedalling with higher power than everyone else.

Increase your pedaling cadence, Sof! The little voice in my head started to ring.

Increasing pedaling cadence sounds simple, but it actually takes months or even years to perfect. If I was riding with a high cadence of above 100 in an easy gear, pedaling at that rate was definitely going to tax my cardiovascular and respiratory system.

If I was fit enough, I knew I could probably hold a high cadence for quite a long time, at least for the entire stretch of almost 20 kilometres! This definitely produced less strain on my muscles. Against the headwinds, I continued riding and sitting upright at a comfortable speed of about 26 kilometres per hour.

Cruising the stretch of highway with a cadence of about 90, I got my non-driving left leg to move faster on my left pedal as my right foot was starting to give me a little problem. I was not too eager to go all out on the bike course.

On the return route, before the final climb on the bridge, I could see many athletes struggling to finish the last 20 kilometres. The heat was expected as athletes stopped at every aid station for hydration. With temperature of about 32 degree Celsius, cramps hit me in the midst of my ride and I had to ease off from my heavier gears. Fatigue was setting in. At every aid station, I took time to pour water down my head, and took in more salt tablets than usual.

At about seven kilometres near the bike finish, I had both my legs burnt, and they cramped up. As I wondered if I could uncleat my shoes then, a security guard came over and asked if I was alright. I stopped my bike totally, gave him a thumbs up, and then walked the cramps off. Fortunately it worked. With a higher cadence at a lower gear, I completed the 90 kilometres safely, with some cross-country terrains near the bike finish. My ride on the course felt like a training ride, complete with spins, climbs, and power interval rides. And with the completion of a challenging century ride with sharp descents, climbs of increasing gradients up the hills, strong headwinds, heat and rain in Ipoh Malaysia just a few weeks ago, I definitely felt the bike course in Cebu easier.

I had lots of time to finish my run. With 75 percent maximum heart beat rate, I was not panting as much as I did in Da Nang. I was taking it easy, walking under some shades and exposed parts of the road, and enjoying the atmosphere of villagers and street kids who laid along the entire road, standing and cheering for us.

When I was running out under the hot sun, I was almost closing my eyes and running calmly. At every aid station, I was picking up a cold bottle of water or placing a huge piece of ice next to my chest. I was overtaking at least more than twenty athletes. After running for about 15 kilometres, I was cheering the slower runners. I could see the pain in their faces.

At the last five kilometres, I was following this guy who was running at a comfortable pace of about 6.5 minutes per kilometre. I just wanted to finish the run. At my last 50 metres, I sprinted across the finishing line, with cramps in my knees. Cebu Philippines Ironman 70.3 – I completed it. This was one endurance race which exposed all your weakness, right to your core of whether you could swim, ride or run.

After completing a few 70.3s, I had two female friends who wanted to sign up for Bintan Ironman 70.3. While one was a fit marathoner, the other was a deaf athlete. Both shared about their fear for the Bintan Hills. We had long discussions and persuasions to go for this race.

"Ultimately your progress in training and completing the race depends more on your attitude and your proper state of mind than on ability and strength", I advised.

A short pause came before the girls decided to commit to the race. This also marked a challenge for me to see them through the race.

"Since you are spending your time with the girls at Bintan, would you want to join Bintan Ironman 70.3?" Richard raised a sudden question to me.

Here came the drug I could not resist. The proximity of the race, the familiarity of the roads, the price of the race --- Richard did make a lot of sense.

Bintan was the same place which I started my first half iron-distance triathlon. It was also this place where I was also having my first training in Bintan when my grandma passed away.

Bintan Ironman 70.3 was happening in less than two weeks after Cebu Ironman 70.3.

Being ready for the 70.3 did not just involve being physically fit. It was also about learning how to handle the bike during occasion of tyre puncture or mechanical fault.

Shifting the chainring and cog while removing the wheel, releasing the tyre and removing the tube, checking the tyre, replacing and inflating the tube – there sure was a lot of finagling, pulling, wiggling, reversing efforts involved. It took me thirty minutes for my first attempt to figure it all out. That was my last training before my race. Thank god I did not have an appointment with my manicurist.

Having made 75 percent to 85 percent maximum heart rate efforts in training or racing, I could see the fruits of those efforts with improved cycling times and higher tolerance level running under the sun. However, racing almost every week before the final 70.3 race of the year did cause some effects on me. I was feeling the stiffness, and the muscle aches all over my body. So on this final week before the final 70.3 of the year, I had to follow a recovery programme, which included lots of nutrition, rest and massage.

On race day, the reminiscence of my last three 70.3 races for the year vanished. I was focused only on the day's racing. There was a slight haze in Bintan, and that had affected my breathing a little.

Richard and I could have booked a hotel room and stayed in our own room for a race. This time round, we decided to share a room with our two friends, took turns to use the shower, and waited one another for breakfast while practicing for cycling rides. All of us knew that in just a few hours, we would be undergoing the grueling race. But none of us mentioned any of this. The carbo-loading affair was also a simple spread and a quiet one.

Bintan 70.3 started with the swim as a shallow but calm start. With the shallow end of the swim, our running on the waters slowed down the swim times as we made our entry to the transition. Being familiar with Bintan, I knew the race has just begun, and pacing was critical.

Despite this, I cycled towards and out of the resort area feeling pretty tired. My body was just not feeling up to it yet. In the first 30 kilometres, I did not ride well. I had the speed, conservative by nature, but the tactics I used were probably dodgy. I only had one strategy – to go slow at the first third, driving up the speed later in the race.

The bike course in Bintan had not much changed. They had proven the same challenges as it had always been. Going all out on the bike course could be deadly as the final 10 kilometres was an uphill. I was fortunate that I still had it in me as I rode through the final distance.

Running the three loops around the lake in Bintan proved to be too much of a bore for me. Though there was shade at certain areas, it was definitely hot out there with sponges, ice, and water thrown everywhere at aid stations. It also lacked supporters on the course.

I walked pretty much on my first loop as I could feel my cramps arising from my earlier ride. I had a few good friends who paced for me on my second loop. Because Cathelin and Gil knew that we were racing for Bintan Ironman 70.3, we were appreciative that they took their time and effort here to support us. Their presence in our second and final loop of the run helped. Nevertheless, I completed the race.

I finished the race feeling hungry, and I took a few pieces of watermelon at the finish line. I sat down, packed my transition stuff into my bag, and started to feel breathless and sick. One athlete of whom I could not recognise walk over, shared about where he saw me on the bike leg, feeling amazed at how a small body frame like me could climb up the hills, and congratulated me. After that, I felt dizzy as I shared the lift with over ten athletes and several bikes.

Upon rushing to my room, I started to vomit. I suspected the watermelon slices, which were out there for hours, created such high lactic acid concentrations in my stomach til they literally made me sick. I fell so sick that I had to be rushed to a nearby clinic for food poisoning. I also postponed my departure from the island the next morning.

While one of my friends suffered from her untimely monthly menses, and was not comfortable to going ahead for the race, the other friend of mine completed her first half iron-distance triathlon race.

I sowed not only a string of continuous action in weekly swims, training rides, and long runs, but I also reaped a certain character. By then, I had welcomed suffering as part of all of us going through such that I started to test myself.

No matter what is going to happen, I have to learn to embrace it, accept it, even though my body or my mind is telling me to quit. Life works such that when we are no longer challenged, we are bored and we don't have much to look forward to, we feel it is hard to keep going and everything feels futile. To fuel my passion growing, I keep exploring for new things to learn. Learning invigorates my soul. I too was looking for my recovery.

Richard and I did something unexpected. We took a vacation to Penang Malaysia to visit his brother. Our vacation while meeting up with families often includes looking for a hotel with a gym, pool, running trails, and ensuring our rented car could carry our bike boxes.

Known as the 'Pearl of the Orient', the island of Penang is famous for its fusion of east and west, new and old, with a landscape brimming with tradition, culture and amazing local cuisine. In a rugged and old Malaysian town, Penang consists of hilly roads, stops at traffic lights and various road conditions.

Rather than bringing my usual Milou, I brought my old aluminium heavy friend, Vitesse, with a 50/34 chain rings, 12/25 rear cassette and smaller 650c wheels. As compared to Milou, Vitesse has a lower number of teeth on its cog. So, the big question was whether Vitesse could ride up the Penang Hills.

With my Penang cycling group of friends campaigning for a cycling lane, we joined in and did our 88-kilometre ride through some incredible riding terrains with snaking coastal roads, beautiful climbs through their local farms and steep pitches through the plantation routes. Amidst all these grinding up the slope, I found the fun factor back again. At that moment when I reached the top of the hill, I turned back to look at the long stretch of highways and mountains around me. I felt invincible.

Heading down the hills was the reward after the strain of riding to the top. While there were many cyclists resting and taking a drink at the top, the journey down the winding road was not for the faint-hearted. It was a collection of dips and turns, and the added danger of cycling right towards a road open to opposing vehicles. We rode through Penang's beautiful towns, charming colonial buildings and serene hilly plantations. What was probably the most exhilarating were the views of the dam and the temple, before descending into the busy town. Each descent required 100 percent concentration and attention at every moment and every curve. I did not rush to challenge these cyclists or exceed 50 kilometres per hour. I was holding my brakes intermittently to control my bike as I went down the hills and turns. With the wind brushing every part of my body, my brain was fully engaged of turning and keeping the bike going while reaching the bottom of the hill safely. This four-hour ride was not planned but we definitely found the high fun factor.

❖

We all recognise training can be time-consuming. But it does not have to negatively impact our work, family time or social life. It wasn't always easy, waking up at five in the morning to get my training done before Richard woke up, or sometimes having to cut short a workout to submit a piece of work needed. My mum also knew I would make it up to her by taking her out for a post-training lunch.

Unless I set a day like a rest day or a recovery workout, the key workouts were made to be specific to the demands of an "A" race. If a goal were to run a 7 minutes per kilometre pace, I would have done a lot of that paced running, not 8 minutes per kilometre in consideration of economical running.

While bike racing and triathlons were aerobic events, bike racing like the one I did for Century rides and Tour de Bintan allowed me to spend time in the drops of my handlebars for racing and pedaling economy. They could use a different set of muscles, which could consume a huge anaerobic component critical for success. I would typically do about two key workouts in a week during the initial phases, which were specific to the demands of the "A" race. The training volume, just like how life had thrown me at any given time, would include several intensities.

I just had to deal with them.

❖

I am a triathlete with driven personalities. After a series of races, I recognised that life gave me opportunities to keep exploring and learning about the sport and the lessons behind them. The sport allowed me to discuss the merits and pitfalls of doing new and old races, and to reconnect with friends. I might not have won the World Championship, but I had won the numerous opportunities to pass down my knowledge in the sport. And I always welcome anyone who lends a listening ear to the Iron Spirit.

Fear often stops us from moving forward. In my journey to Sydney for my race in Western Sydney Ironman 70.3, I explored something different. I wanted to travel there alone. While there might be initial fear, I still did it anyway. Richard and I did not travel together for this trip.

It was this period that I reminisced how much teamwork Richard and I had forged together – sharing a meal on board together, reading the map, directing the driver, and checking for restaurants. Before departure, I could not say I was missing him. It was until I ordered a piece of cheesecake and coffee sitting and staring at them alone at the café of the departure hall of the airport that I started to find something missing. I was actually missing him. I guessed this was what doing something different had brought to me.

Western Sydney Ironman 70.3 was a race where I experienced all climates. It started with a drizzle in my non-wetsuit swim in the iconic Penrith Lake home to the 2000 Olympic Sydney International Regatta Center. It then proceeded to a cool breezy bike ride along the bumpy countryside roads and tight u-turns, and then followed with a hot sunny run around the Penrith Lake at the end. Although we faced different weather along the course, I encouraged a few Japanese athletes along the way. Surprisingly, it was my best 70.3 for the year. That year, I received the Ironman Bronze All World Athlete (AWA) title. I felt honoured to be one of the 23,500 athletes receiving the AWA title for the year 2015.

I felt honoured to run so near to the 2000 Olympic Sydney Penrith Lake.

As the year ended, Richard and I remembered how we had lost a couple of our dear ones throughout the year, and had learnt to cherish one another more. We had read about a few new interesting developments in overseas sport facilities. We also wanted to travel to The States as a married couple for a long time. It was easy to find a thousand excuses to put all these plans off, complain about it, and worry about this and that.

It was now timely for us to visit Thanyapura Phuket, well known for its sports facilities. We made our way there, and participated in a challenging 8-kilometre trail run, consisting of 200 percent grade climbs. This was my greatest eye-opener in terms of trail runs, or rather climbs literally.

I rode up one of the steep challenging sections of Phuket hills.

After which, I wondered how much more crazy Richard and I could get! We flew more than 24 hours from Singapore to San Francisco, and each bought a bike first thing when we reached San Francisco. It made absolute sense for us to buy as it was much cheaper than for us to rent the bikes. We cycled around San Francisco, across The Golden Gates to the other island near Richardson Bay, before returning to the city to complete The Golden Gates Half Marathon the next day. We then went on a road trip, driving more than 18 hours to Las Vegas, and cycled around The Red Rock Canyon, Scenic Drive, and Dams the subsequent few days. Of course, we too completed the Las Vegas Rock n Roll 5K and Half Marathon under the cold rainy weather.

I enjoyed cycling around The Golden Gates San Francisco.

I also cycled around The Red Rock Canyon in Las Vegas.

Life was not just about races. We enjoyed the best sights in America and made a couple of new friends. We grabbed the opportunity when Celine Dion returned to the stage, and we snapped up the tickets to watch her grand performance for the night.

I believe that anyone can do a half iron-distance triathlon or even a full iron-distance triathlon. It is work, commitment, and perseverance. And still it must be fun. Race day is that single day, the culmination of several days before the next one, and it brings its own little joy and celebration for every challenge I undergo.

CONCLUSION

MOVING FORWARD IN LIFE

After all these races, I heard many athletes talking about qualifying for Kona or some specific World Championship. After learning of the end of the existing ballot system and that athletes would need to win races to qualify to go to Kona, I asked Richard if I would ever have a chance.

I could find the most well-known coach or the most competent triathlon club, or even take a few years off from work and train hard, so that someday – who knows when – my chance will come. But then, what's next?

After racing several triathlons, I had come to realise that getting to race in Kona was no longer as important as the practice of the Iron Spirit itself. No matter how long or how hard I train, how many races I participate in, there is a lifetime of study, experience, and practice in every one of them and ahead of me.

Challenges in races are there for a reason. I have stopped complaining about the waters, the hills, or the terrains. It was all about signing up for an activity - I commit, train hard, be humble, don't complain, and do my best in every one of them, both physically and mentally.

I want picking up the finisher medal to be more than simply a piece of merchandise I paid for in my race registration. If not, I would be like many of the athletes who treat long distance triathlon races as just a check off the bucket list.

The completion of a full iron-distance triathlon was not the end of anything. Really. My story may or may not be encouraging for some people who want to beat their own challenges in their lives in one way or another.

Then what about the people who were not doing as well, who have tried, and who lacked the energy to continue to fight and those who just find no purpose in doing so? Those people who are living in their own world, not responding, or struggling to face something that they never wanted to hear?

I cannot help them with the problem of listening to themselves, and I cannot change the basics of what was happening around them. In the end, all I can do is to try to encourage them to realise their attitude, and try to talk about what their environment *could not* do, and probably what they *could* do.

I imagine that there is nothing quite like a view of the earth from outer space which reminds me consistently how small a problem we are facing in the grand scheme of things in the universe. Yet no matter how I rationalise the many tasks on hand we do, we continually get stuck thinking we have all the answers.

The fact is we don't. No one has the right answers. We live and work in an uncertain world where everything can change in an instant. This is life. As much as we would like to plan and chart our directions going forward, the world continues to surprise us, and situations will arise in which we do not know what to do the next moment.

I started to bring my mum out for races,
so that she could refocus her energies in the right places.
Sometimes it works, sometimes it doesn't. Life still
goes on. And that's Mum, alright.

Faith is a willingness to acknowledge that things happen for a reason. The experiences I have encountered in my life have somehow given me faith. With faith, I know that there is something greater at work, something more to learn, some reason for the unwanted outcome that has not yet revealed itself. I acknowledge it is done on my behalf and for my benefit.

It allows the faithful to move beyond judgment, blame, self-pity to look for what is needed now and what can be learned later. Faith reminds me that when I do my best and try my hardest but things still don't go the way I expected, there is a reason; something better or different needs to occur. Faith has lifted me above despair and disappointment and opens my eyes to hope.

Wherever we are in our life, whether we are running away from it or not, we can make a choice to be an athlete. If no one defines us as athletes, we adopt that mindset, and we make it as our own defining essence. We are "born with" it, and so we live with it. I made my choice, took up that mindset, and that has allowed me to move towards a new level of achievement.

Life in itself is a process, a challenge and an opportunity that is open to everyone in this journey. Whether we are happy or sad, we have to live it. Laying out the programs, the races, the tricks, the mechanics, the physiology and psychology - Life has given a chance for us to live this journey.

Many people live a life where they have to see it to believe it. But my proven point is that I did imagine it; I believed in it and lived probably half my life to see it. Life has given a vast paradise, waiting for me to explore. The aches and the pains are what life has given us. But over the course of time, with strength, form, and training that I have undertaken, I learnt to eliminate these ailments, learnt to love one another, learnt to love ourselves, have more fun in life, and achieve performance enhancements towards life.

At the lowest points in my life, be it not being able to get a job, or when my dear ones passed away or myself having to overcome an illness or a fear of my own, no one is going to care how many marathons or triathlon races I have completed or how tough I am. There would be people who would look at me with pathetic eyes or with condolences.

These could beat me down flat and I could either stay that way permanently, or I could stand up and keep moving forward.

Just three months ago, Richard bought a triathlon bike for me. We are anticipating the excitement and fun I would have racing the year forward should I be able to ride on a triathlon bike. I am looking forward to ride my few-month-old pretty pink and blue Giant Liv triathlon bike. To stay strong in my Iron Spirit belief, I named my bike "Beliv".

I could choose to stop writing now, or I keep moving forward.

Here I am pushing Beliv out of the house as I make my way onto the roads. I want to succeed as long as I can breathe right here, right now.

Top 10 Observations and Options in My Triathlon Journey

Think before Act

1   Clincher versus Tubular Wheels

Once we make our case – learning a skill, racing, winning – we gather key facts about the environment and work in favour of them. I made my choice of clincher over tubular wheels because of its low cost, ease of maintenance and change of tyre.

Prioritise

2   Road Bike versus Triathlon Bike

Start with what you know. In general, road bike is good for hilly course whereas a triathlon bike is fine for flatter course. While a triathlon bike puts a cyclist at a more forward position, enabling the cyclist to be in a more aerodynamic position, a road bike corners, handles better and climbs more efficiently.

If I were to join both triathlon and road races, and I only have one choice of bike, it is definitely the road bike. I have great difficulty in getting a triathlon bike for a person of my height and with a short inseam. Therefore, I will always go for the bike with the best fit.

3 Brands, Material, Weight of Bikes and Aerodynamics

Different brands offer different geometry for different people. Certain materials such as carbon do offer more comfort than aluminium but they come with a price. At the end of the day, I go for the one that I can afford with an ultimate choice of comfort and fit.

4 Standard bottles versus Aero bottles on Bikes

My choice is standard bottles. All customised aero bottles and cages are more expensive. Standard ones allow easy change of bike bottles during races, rather than having to fill the bottles with the hydration.

5 One piece tri suit versus two piece of tri suit

A two-piece tri suit provides versatility, ease and convenience whenever I go to the loo. But a one-piece tri suit offers a streamlined and aerodynamic fit. One-piece tri suit also does not allow the top to ride up. The more important consideration is to choose a quality tri-suit with durable fabric (that does not thin out too soon!), and seams and comfortable cycling pad that do not chafe.

6 Saddle

This is a very personal item. What suits one person may not fit another. With my bike fitter, I have the best opportunities to try some of the most expensive saddles. My advice is not to head out to buy the most expensive saddle or follow what another friend has told you about the best saddle he had. A good consideration is to borrow the saddle from a friend and try it yourself first.

Manage a Crisis

7   Hand pump versus CO2 pump on bike

CO2 enables much faster inflation than a hand pump. More effort
is required to remove the hand pump from the bike and to pump the
same amount of air into the tyre than that of a CO2. And a hand
pump can never reach as high a psi as a CO2 does.

8   Gels versus Natural Foods

Our bodies burn carbohydrates and fats when we exercise. The faster
we go, the more carbs we burn with respect to our fat stores. I don't
usually use gels during most training sessions. Unless I need a quick
replacement of glycogen, I prefer gels because they are denser and
release energy faster during races. However, I can stomach only certain
brands of gels. The other main reason is also because I just somehow
cannot bite my food during races.

Raise a Red Flag

9   Contact Lens versus Prescribed Glasses

While contact lenses allowed me to wear any shades and goggles, one
has to be careful of hygiene and sufficient time for eyes to rest. In
long distance triathlons, this may not be healthy. Due to the medical
condition of my eye, I cannot wear contact lenses. Therefore I have to
wear optical goggles and shades with prescribed inserts.

10 Rest versus Training

I started out the sport with nothing. I then learned to move my legs at
a faster speed. I stayed focus on improving all my triathlon disciplines

including nutrition. I learnt to swim and ride efficiently, transiting and holding it all together in my run.

With all the commitment invested in the sport and the desire to improve, these strengths also become an athlete's greatest weaknesses. With all the best bikes, equipment, and time invested in racing their best races, athletes end up feeling the fatigue and monotony of the sport. Tapering and recovery are keys to prevent withdrawal syndrome. Those one or two days of rest will not make you any weaker in your sport if you have a training program in place.

Some of the Interesting Pros
I met in My Learning Journey

I met different people in my journey. Along the way, I made a quick chat with some of these Pros and picked up key lessons to move forward in life.

1   Be Prepared to Push Yourself Through

Robbie McEwen, an Australian former professional road bicycle racer, prepared himself for the Worlds by pushing himself through the Tours, so that he could earn his rest and build up towards the Worlds. Sprinting helps in confidence as there is no room for self-doubt and going through the gap that only you can see.

2   Never Doubt Yourself

Pro Triathlete, Luke McKenzie and I met at training run years ago. I was just starting to be a triathlete. He was a rookie in the sport.

The running group was divided into three smaller groups ranging from slower ones to the faster ones. I saw Luke as a humble athlete who carries a lot of faith on himself. Luke shared his dreams on going to Kona. In 2013, he won second in Kona.

3   Pushing Beyond Limits

There is no coincidence in life. Ultramarathoner and mountaineer, Kilian Jornet lived in the mountains and loved the mountains since young.

Kilian loves chocolate with milk. Find a motivation. Chocolates now become a gentle reminder for me on how Kilian has kept himself motivated with the different challenges.

4   Love Exists in all Humans

I looked at Caroline Steffen, this Pro triathlete with a tall body built and I thought, I should give her a music CD for her birthday. It was accompanied with a letter of encouragement and story about my personal loss.

After the race, Caroline walked over to me and amicably gave me a hug. We all understood how much the hug meant to us. We were different yet we were so similar in a way that it had been trying times for us all. I looked at this lady. Xena with some weird force that was so much more powerful than myself moved me to be as strong as she is.

5   Family Matters

No amount of money would pay you enough to sacrifice your time with your loved ones. Craig Alexander's success in his sports comes from the motivation he derives from his family. With experience, we all learn to deal with life better and always come out stronger.

6   Make a Difference

Racing internationally for years, Chris Lieto has competed in the most beautiful countries in the world. Often hidden behind these scenic vast lands are children and families living in poverty. Chris makes a difference to these children's lives by giving back to society. Leave a footprint whenever we go. When asked if he would race in Kona again, his reply was "He is happy making a positive difference to these kids".

Here were some of the interesting professionals I met in my journey